HEALTH CARE ISSUES, COSTS AND ACCESS

FRAUD DETECTION AND DETERRENCE IN MEDICARE AND MEDICAID

HEALTH CARE ISSUES, COSTS AND ACCESS

Additional books in this series can be found on Nova's website
under the Series tab.

Additional e-books in this series can be found on Nova's website
under the e-book tab.

HEALTH CARE ISSUES, COSTS AND ACCESS

FRAUD DETECTION AND DETERRENCE IN MEDICARE AND MEDICAID

ANTON FERILLI
EDITOR

nova publishers
New York

For permission to use material from this book please contact us:
Telephone 631-231-7269; Fax 631-231-8175
Web Site: http://www.novapublishers.com

Library of Congress Cataloging-in-Publication Data

ISBN: 978-1-62417-658-6

Published by Nova Science Publishers, Inc. ✝ New York

CONTENTS

PREFACE

The Government Accountability Office (GAO) has designated Medicare and Medicaid as high-risk programs, in part due to their susceptibility to improper payments--estimated to be about $70 billion in fiscal year 2010. Improper payments have many causes, such as submissions of duplicate claims or fraud, waste, and abuse. As the administrator of these programs, the Centers for Medicare and Medicaid Services (CMS) is responsible for safeguarding them from loss. This book explores fraud detection and deterrence in Medicare and Medicaid, with a focus on fraud detection systems; screening providers and suppliers; and program integrity.

Chapter 1 – GAO has designated Medicare and Medicaid as high-risk programs, in part due to their susceptibility to improper payments—estimated to be about $70 billion in fiscal year 2010. Improper payments have many causes, such as submissions of duplicate claims or fraud, waste, and abuse. As the administrator of these programs, the Centers for Medicare and Medicaid Services (CMS) is responsible for safeguarding them from loss. To integrate claims information and improve its ability to detect fraud, waste, and abuse in these programs, CMS initiated two information technology system programs: the Integrated Data Repository (IDR) and One Program Integrity (One PI).

GAO was asked to (1) assess the extent to which IDR and One PI have been developed and implemented and (2) determine CMS's progress toward achieving its goals and objectives for using these systems to help detect fraud, waste, and abuse. To do so, GAO reviewed system and program management plans and other documents and compared them to key practices. GAO also interviewed program officials, analyzed system data, and reviewed reported costs and benefits.

Chapter 2 – This is the Background Memo for the Hearing on "Medicare Contractors' Efforts to Fight Fraud: Moving Beyond 'Pay and Chase'" by House Committee on Energy and Commerce, Subcommittee on Oversight and Investigations.

Chapter 3 – GAO has designated Medicare as a high-risk program. Since 1990, every two years GAO has provided Congress with an update on this program, which highlights government operations that are at high risk for waste, fraud, abuse mismanagement or in need of broad reform. Medicare has been included in this program in part because its complexity makes it particularly vulnerable to fraud. Fraud involves an intentional act or representation to deceive with the knowledge that the action or representation could result in gain. The deceptive nature of fraud makes its extent in the Medicare program difficult to measure in a reliable way, but it is clear that fraud contributes to Medicare's fiscal problems. Reducing fraud could help rein in the escalating costs of the program.

This statement focuses on the progress made and important steps to be taken by CMS and its program integrity contractors to reduce fraud in Medicare. These contractors perform functions such as screening and enrolling providers, detecting and investigating potential fraud, and identifying improper payments and vulnerabilities that could lead to payment errors. This statement is based on relevant GAO products and recommendations issued from 2004 through 2012 using a variety of methodologies, such as analyses of Medicare claims, review of relevant policies and procedures, and interviews with officials.

Chapter 4 – This is the Statement of Ted Doolittle, Deputy Director, Center for Program Integrity, Department of Health and Human Services.

Chapter 5 – This is the Testimony of Robert A. Vito, Regional Inspector General, U.S. Department of Health and Human Services.

Chapter 6 – According to the Centers for Medicare & Medicaid Services (CMS)—the agency within the Department of Health and Human Services (HHS) that administers the Medicare program—more than 1.5 million health providers and suppliers of medical equipment were enrolled in the Medicare program in 2011, and 30,000 more enroll each month. CMS has established Medicare enrollment standards and procedures intended to ensure that only qualified providers and suppliers can enroll. While most providers and suppliers pose a limited risk to the Medicare program, our previous work found persistent weaknesses in CMS's Medicare enrollment standards and procedures that increased the risk of enrolling entities intent on defrauding the program. In 2010, the Patient Protection and Affordable Care Act (PPACA) authorized CMS to implement procedures to strengthen the Medicare enrollment process.

GAO was asked to review CMS's Medicare provider enrollment procedures. In this chapter, GAO describes (1) how CMS and its contractors use provider and supplier enrollment information to prevent improper payments and factors that may affect the usefulness of this information, and (2) the extent to which CMS has implemented new provider and supplier enrollment screening procedures since the enactment of PPACA. To do so, GAO reviewed relevant regulations and documents, and interviewed officials from CMS and a sample of four of the agency's contractors based on the volume of claims they processed and the status of their contracts with CMS.

Chapter 7 – In 2011, CMS estimated that Medicaid and Medicare had improper payments of $21.9 billion and almost $43 billion, respectively—among the largest for all federal programs. Both health care programs are on GAO's list of high-risk programs. Over the years, Congress has passed legislation designed to help address program integrity issues in the two programs but they remain vulnerable to fraud, waste, and abuse. The program integrity challenges are different for Medicaid and Medicare. With 51 distinct state-based programs, Medicaid has complex challenges for finding the appropriate balance between state and federal efforts. Medicare uses contractors to help administer the program and CMS must oversee their efforts. This statement examines the progress made and important steps still to be taken in these programs. GAO focused on four key strategies and recommendations that were designed to facilitate them that were identified in prior work and that could help reduce improper payments: (1) strengthening provider enrollment standards and procedures to ensure that only legitimate providers participate in the program; (2) improving prepayment controls; (3) improving postpayment claims review and recovery of improper payments; and (4) developing a robust process for addressing identified vulnerabilities. This statement is based on GAO products issued from April 2004 through May 2012 and interviews with agency officials and other stakeholders. In May 2012, GAO also received additional information from CMS on agency actions. GAO received technical comments from CMS officials and incorporated them into this statement.

Chapter 8 – This is the Statement of Dr. Peter Budetti, Director, Center for Program Integrity, Department of Health and Human Services.

In: Fraud Detection and Deterrence ... ISBN: 978-1-62417-658-6
Editor: Anton Ferilli

Chapter 1

FRAUD DETECTION SYSTEMS: CENTERS FOR MEDICARE AND MEDICAID SERVICES NEEDS TO ENSURE MORE WIDESPREAD USE*

United States Government Accountability Office

WHY GAO DID THIS STUDY

GAO has designated Medicare and Medicaid as high-risk programs, in part due to their susceptibility to improper payments—estimated to be about $70 billion in fiscal year 2010. Improper payments have many causes, such as submissions of duplicate claims or fraud, waste, and abuse. As the administrator of these programs, the Centers for Medicare and Medicaid Services (CMS) is responsible for safeguarding them from loss. To integrate claims information and improve its ability to detect fraud, waste, and abuse in these programs, CMS initiated two information technology system programs: the Integrated Data Repository (IDR) and One Program Integrity (One PI).

GAO was asked to (1) assess the extent to which IDR and One PI have been developed and implemented and (2) determine CMS's progress toward achieving its goals and objectives for using these systems to help detect fraud,

---

* This is an edited, reformatted and augmented version of United States Government Accountability Office Publication No. GAO-11-475, dated June 2011.

waste, and abuse. To do so, GAO reviewed system and program management plans and other documents and compared them to key practices. GAO also interviewed program officials, analyzed system data, and reviewed reported costs and benefits.

What GAO Recommends

GAO is recommending that CMS take steps to finalize plans and reliable schedules for fully implementing and expanding the use of the systems and to define measurable benefits. In its comments, CMS concurred with GAO's recommendations.

What GAO Found

CMS has developed and begun using both IDR and One PI, but has not incorporated into IDR all data as planned and has not taken steps to ensure widespread use of One PI to enhance efforts to detect fraud, waste, and abuse. IDR is intended to be the central repository of Medicare and Medicaid data needed to help CMS program integrity staff and contractors prevent and detect improper payments of Medicare and Medicaid claims.

Program integrity analysts use these data to identify patterns of unusual activities or transactions that may indicate fraudulent charges or other types of improper payments. IDR has been operational and in use since September 2006. However, it does not include all the data that were planned to be incorporated by fiscal year 2010. For example, IDR includes most types of Medicare claims data, but not the Medicaid data needed to help analysts detect improper payments of Medicaid claims. IDR also does not include data from other CMS systems that are needed to help analysts prevent improper payments, such as information about claims at the time they are filed and being processed.

According to program officials, these data were not incorporated because of obstacles introduced by technical issues and delays in funding. Further, the agency has not finalized plans or developed reliable schedules for efforts to incorporate these data. Until it does so, CMS may face additional delays in making available all the data that are needed to support enhanced program integrity efforts.

One PI is a Web-based portal that is to provide CMS staff and contractors with a single source of access to data contained in IDR, as well as tools for analyzing those data.

While One PI has been developed and deployed to users, few program integrity analysts were trained and using the system. Specifically, One PI program officials planned for 639 program integrity analysts to be using the system by the end of fiscal year 2010; however, as of October 2010, only 41—less than 7 percent—were actively using the portal and tools. According to program officials, the agency's initial training plans were insufficient and, as a result, they were not able to train the intended community of users. Until program officials finalize plans and develop reliable schedules for training users and expanding the use of One PI, the agency may continue to experience delays in reaching widespread use and determining additional needs for full implementation of the system.

While CMS has made progress toward its goals to provide a single repository of data and enhanced analytical capabilities for program integrity efforts, the agency is not yet positioned to identify, measure, and track benefits realized from its efforts. As a result, it is unknown whether IDR and One PI as currently implemented have provided financial benefits. According to IDR officials, they do not measure benefits realized from increases in the detection rate for improper payments because they rely on business owners to do so, and One PI officials stated that, because of the limited use of the system, there are not enough data to measure and gauge the program's success toward achieving the $21 billion in financial benefits that the agency projected.

ABBREVIATIONS

CMS	Centers for Medicare and Medicaid Services
HHS	Department of Health and Human Services
HIPAA	Health Insurance Portability and Accountability Act
IDR	Integrated Data Repository
IT	information technology
MACBIS	Medicaid and Children's Health Insurance Program Business Information and Solutions
OIG	Office of the Inspector General
OMB	Office of Management and Budget
One PI	One Program Integrity

The Honorable Thomas R. Carper
Chairman
Subcommittee on Federal Financial Management, Government Information, Federal Services, and International Security Committee on Homeland Security and Governmental Affairs
United States Senate

The Honorable Scott Brown
Ranking Member
Subcommittee on Federal Financial Management, Government Information, Federal Services, and International Security Committee on Homeland Security and Governmental Affairs
United States Senate

The Honorable John McCain
United States Senate

For more than 20 years, GAO has designated Medicare as a high-risk program due to its size and complexity, as well as its susceptibility to mismanagement and improper payments. Improper payments are overpayments or underpayments that should not have been made or were made in an incorrect amount.[1] Improper payments may be due to errors, such as the inadvertent submission of duplicate claims for the same service, or misconduct, such as fraud and abuse. Since 2003, we have also designated Medicaid as a high-risk program because of concerns about the adequacy of its fiscal oversight, which is necessary to prevent inappropriate spending. The Department of Health and Human Services (HHS) reported about $70 billion in improper payments for the Medicare and Medicaid programs in fiscal year 2010.

The Centers for Medicare and Medicaid Services (CMS) within HHS is responsible for administering the Medicare and Medicaid programs and leading efforts to reduce improper payments. As part of these efforts, CMS conducts reviews to prevent improper payments before claims are paid and reviews of claims potentially paid in error. These activities are predominantly carried out by contractors who, along with CMS personnel, use various information technology (IT) solutions to consolidate and analyze data in support of efforts to detect improper payments of claims. For example, these analysts may use software tools to access data about claims to identify patterns of unusual activities by attempting to match services with patients' diagnoses.

In 2006, CMS initiated efforts to centralize and make more accessible the data needed to conduct these analyses, and to improve the analytical tools available to its own and contractor analysts. Among these initiatives are the Integrated Data Repository (IDR), which is intended to provide a single source of data related to Medicare and Medicaid claims, and the One Program Integrity (One PI) system, a Web-based portal[2] and suite of analytical software tools used to extract data from IDR and enable complex analyses of these data.

You asked us to examine CMS's efforts to develop and implement IDR and One PI to improve the agency's ability to detect fraud, waste, and abuse in administering these programs. Specifically, our objectives were to

1) assess the extent to which the IDR and One PI systems have been developed and implemented, and
2) determine the agency's progress toward achieving defined goals and objectives for using the systems to help detect fraud, waste, and abuse in the Medicare and Medicaid programs.

To address these objectives, we reviewed IDR and One PI program management and planning documentation and held discussions with agency officials and system users. Specifically, to assess the extent to which IDR and One PI have been developed and implemented, we compared the functionality that has been implemented to date to estimated schedule milestones and performance measures. We also reviewed the programs' requirements development and management plans and other project management artifacts and assessed CMS's documented processes against criteria established by the Software Engineering Institute.[3] To supplement the information we collected from agency documents, we met with agency officials to discuss plans for and management of the IDR and One PI programs.

To determine the agency's progress toward achieving goals and objectives for improving outcomes of its program integrity initiatives, we reviewed agencywide strategic plans and program planning documents to identify the goals and objectives, and assessed the extent to which IDR and One PI supported efforts to achieve them. We also interviewed agency officials about steps the agency had taken to achieve the goals and objectives. To determine the extent to which the use of IDR and One PI has enabled the agency to meet goals for improving its ability to detect fraud, waste, and abuse, we identified CMS program integrity personnel and contractors who actively use the systems by analyzing training information and system login data. We then held discussions with groups of these users to determine the extent to which and for what purposes they used the system. We also compared reported system costs and financial benefits to those projected for both IDR and One PI.

We assessed the reliability of the agency's data related to project management practices; cost, schedule, and financial benefit estimates; and system usage through interviews with agency officials knowledgeable of the management of the programs, methods for tracking and reporting costs of the IDR and One PI programs, the programs' user community and training plans, and mechanisms for accessing the systems. We determined that the data we collected and assessed were sufficiently reliable for the purposes of our study.

We conducted our work in support of this performance audit primarily at CMS's headquarters in Baltimore, Maryland, from June 2010 to June 2011, in accordance with generally accepted government auditing standards. Those standards require that we plan and perform the audit to obtain sufficient, appropriate evidence to provide a reasonable basis for our findings and conclusions based on our audit objectives. We believe that the evidence obtained provides a reasonable basis for our findings and conclusions based on our audit objectives. Detailed information about our objectives, scope, and methodology is discussed in appendix I.

BACKGROUND

Medicare is a federal program that provides health insurance coverage for individuals aged 65 and older and for certain disabled persons. It is funded by general revenues, payroll taxes paid by most employees, employers, and individuals who are self-employed, and beneficiary premiums. Medicare consists of four parts. Medicare Part A provides payment for inpatient hospital, skilled nursing facility, some home health, and hospice services, while Part B pays for hospital outpatient, physician, some home health, durable medical equipment, and preventive services. In addition, Medicare beneficiaries have an option to participate in Medicare Advantage, also known as Part C, which pays private health plans to provide the services covered by Medicare Parts A and B. Further, all Medicare beneficiaries may purchase coverage for outpatient prescription drugs under Medicare Part D, and some Medicare Advantage plans also include Part D coverage. In 2010, Medicare covered 47 million elderly and disabled beneficiaries and had estimated outlays of about $509 billion.

CMS uses contractors to help administer the claims processing and payment systems for Medicare. These administrative contractors are responsible for processing approximately 4.5 million claims per workday. The contractors review the claims submitted by providers to ensure payment is made only for medically necessary services covered by Medicare for eligible individuals.

Medicaid is the federal-state program that provides health coverage for acute and long-term care services for over 65 million low-income people. It consists of more than 50 distinct state-based programs that each define eligibility requirements and administer payment for health care services for low-income individuals, including children, families, the aged, and the disabled. Within broad federal requirements, each state operates its Medicaid program according to a state plan. Low-income Americans who meet their state's Medicaid eligibility criteria are entitled to have payments made on their behalf for covered services. States are entitled to federal matching funds, which differ from state to state but can be up to three-fourths of their costs of this coverage. The amount paid with federal funds is determined by a formula established in law.[4]

CMS oversees the Medicaid program at the federal level, while the states administer their respective programs' day-to-day operations, such as enrolling eligible individuals, establishing payment amounts for covered benefits, establishing standards for providers and managed care plans, processing and paying for claims and managed care, and ensuring that state and federal health care funds are not spent improperly or diverted by fraudulent providers. The estimated outlays for Medicaid for both the federal and state governments were $408 billion in 2010. Of this cost, approximately $275 billion was incurred by the federal government and $133 billion by the states.

CMS Program Integrity Initiatives

The Health Insurance Portability and Accountability Act (HIPAA) of 1996 established the Medicare Integrity Program to increase and stabilize federal funding for health care antifraud activities.[5] The act appropriated funds for the program as well as amounts for HHS and the Department of Justice to carry out the health care fraud and abuse control program. Subsequent legislation further outlined responsibilities under the Medicare Integrity Program.

Under the Medicare Integrity Program, CMS staff and several types of contractors perform functions to help detect cases of fraud, waste, and abuse, and other payment errors, which include reviews of paid claims to identify patterns of aberrant billing. Among these program integrity contractors are program safeguard contractors, zone program integrity contractors, and Medicare drug integrity contractors.[6] The program safeguard and zone program integrity contractors are responsible for ensuring the integrity of benefit payments for Medicare Parts A and B (including durable medical equipment), as well as the Medi-Medi data match program.[7] Medicare drug integrity contractors are responsible for monitoring fraud, waste, or abuse in the Medicare prescription drug program (i.e., Part D). These contractors work with the HHS Office of the Inspector General (OIG) and law enforcement organizations, such as the Department of Justice, to help law enforcement pursue criminal or civil penalties when fraudulent claims are detected. Table 1 summarizes the origin and responsibilities of the program integrity contractors who help CMS to detect fraud, waste, and abuse.

Table 1. Responsibilities of CMS Program Integrity Contractors

Type of contractor	Origin and scope of responsibility
Program safeguard contractors	Origin: Health Insurance Portability and Accountability Act of 1996, section 202, as amended. Scope of responsibility: Responsible for detecting and deterring fraud and abuse in Medicare Part A and Part B in their 17 jurisdictions.
Zone program integrity contractors	Origin: In response to section 911 of the Medicare Prescription Drug, Improvement, and Modernization Act of 2003. Scope of responsibility: Responsible for performing a wide range of medical review, data analysis, and auditing activities for all Medicare programs within seven geographic regions, or zones.
Medicare drug integrity contractors	Origin: In response to the establishment of the Part D prescription drug benefit program by the Medicare Prescription Drug, Improvement, and Modernization Act of 2003, beginning January 1, 2006. Scope of responsibility: Responsible for monitoring the Medicare Prescription Drug program to detect and deter cases of fraud and abuse.

Source: GAO analysis of CMS data.

In addition to provisions of HIPAA and other legislation intended to strengthen Medicare program integrity functions, in 2006 Congress created the Medicaid Integrity Program through the Deficit Reduction Act of 2005.[8] Its goals are to strengthen the national Medicaid audit program and to enhance federal oversight of and support and assistance to state Medicaid programs. The program provides states with technical assistance and support to enhance the federal-state partnership as well as to expand activities that involve data analysis, sharing algorithms of known improper billings, and fraud awareness through education and outreach. Individual states are responsible for ensuring the accuracy of Medicaid payments within their state programs, which can involve using their own staff or contractors to analyze claims to detect improper payments. In addition to the states' efforts, CMS employs Medicaid program integrity contractors to perform specific activities as part of its efforts to detect fraud, waste, and abuse in the Medicaid program, such as reviewing provider claims payments that have been processed by the states.

Generally, each state Medicaid program integrity unit works independently, using its own data models, data warehouses, and approach to analysis. As a result, Medicaid data are stored in multiple disparate systems and databases throughout the country. Because of the volumes of work, states often augment their in-house capabilities by contracting with companies that specialize in Medicaid claims and utilization reviews. State Medicaid program integrity units target their activities to those providers that pose the greatest financial risk to their Medicaid programs. However, the states have limited methods of identifying Medicaid fraud in neighboring jurisdictions or by providers who move from state to state.

As stated in a July 2007 report by the HHS OIG,[9] the agency intends for program integrity contractors to perform a significant amount of self-initiated, exploratory analysis to seek patterns or instances of fraud and abuse. One of the specific activities undertaken by these contractors is the analysis of claims data to identify improper billing that may indicate fraud or abuse. If the billing appears to be potentially fraudulent or abusive, the contractors take further actions, which can include requesting and reviewing medical records associated with the claims and referring the case to law enforcement.

In 2010, CMS created the Center for Program Integrity to serve as its focal point for all national Medicare and Medicaid program integrity fraud and abuse issues. The new center is responsible for, among other things, collaborating with other CMS components to develop and implement a comprehensive strategic plan, objectives, and measures to carry out the agency's program integrity mission and goals, and ensure program vulnerabilities are identified and resolved. According to agency documentation describing the program, the center was designed to

- promote the integrity of the Medicare and Medicaid programs through provider and contractor audits and policy reviews, identification and monitoring of program vulnerabilities, and support and assistance to states;
- collaborate on the development and advancement of new legislative initiatives and improvements to deter, reduce, and eliminate fraud, waste and abuse;
- oversee all CMS interactions and collaboration with key stakeholders related to program integrity (e.g., the Department of Justice, HHS OIG, and state law enforcement agencies) for the purposes of detecting, deterring, monitoring, and combating fraud and abuse; and
- take action against those who commit or participate in fraudulent or other unlawful activities.

CMS's Use of IT to Help Detect Fraud, Waste, and Abuse

Like financial institutions, credit card companies, telecommunications firms, and other private sector companies that take steps to protect customers' accounts, CMS uses automated software tools to help predict or detect cases of improper claims and payments. For more than a decade, CMS and its contractors have applied such tools to access data from various sources to analyze patterns of unusual activities or financial transactions that may indicate fraudulent charges or other types of improper payments. For example, to identify unusual billing patterns and to support referrals for prosecution or other action, CMS and program integrity contractor analysts and investigators need, among other things, access to information about key actions taken to process claims as they are filed and specific details about claims already paid. This includes information on claims as they are billed, adjusted, and paid or denied; check numbers on payments of claims; and other specific information that could help establish provider intent. These data, along with data on regional or national trends on claims billing and payment, support the investigation and potential prosecution of fraud cases. Upon completing investigations, the contractors determine whether to refer the investigations as cases to law enforcement officials.

CMS and its program integrity contractors currently use many different means to store and manipulate data and, since the establishment of the agency's program integrity initiatives in the 1990s, have built multiple databases and developed analytical software tools to meet their individual and unique needs. However, according to CMS, these geographically distributed, regional approaches to data analysis result in duplicate data and limit the agency's ability to conduct analyses of data on a nationwide basis. Additionally, data on Medicaid claims are scattered among the states in multiple disparate systems and data stores, and are not readily available to CMS. Thus, CMS has been working for most of the past decade to consolidate program integrity data and analytical tools for detecting fraud, waste, and abuse. The agency's efforts led to the initiation of the IDR program and, subsequently, the One PI program, which are intended to provide CMS and its program integrity contractors with a centralized source that consolidates Medicare and Medicaid data from the many disparate and dispersed legacy systems and databases and a Web-based portal and set of analytical tools by which these data can be accessed and analyzed to help detect cases of fraud, waste, and abuse.

CMS's Initiative to Develop a Centralized Source of Medicare and Medicaid Data

The CMS Office of Information Services is responsible for agencywide IT management. Its initiative to develop a centralized data warehouse began in 2003 as an element of the agency's Enterprise Data Modernization strategy. According to agency documentation, the strategy was designed to meet the increasing demand for higher quality and more timely data to support decision making throughout the agency, including identifying trends and discovering patterns of fraud, waste, and abuse. As part of the strategy, the agency established the Data Warehouse Modernization project to develop and implement the technology needed to store longterm data for analytical purposes, such as summary reports and statistical analyses. CMS initially planned for the data warehouse project to be complete by September 30, 2008.

However, in 2006 CMS expanded the scope of the project to not only modernize data storage technology but also to integrate Medicare and Medicaid data into a centralized repository. At that time, program officials also changed the name to IDR, which reflected the expanded scope. The Office of Information Services' Enterprise Data Group manages the IDR program and is responsible for the design and implementation of the system. The program's overall goal is to integrate Medicare and Medicaid data so that CMS and its partners may access the data from a single source. Specific goals for the program are to

- transition from stove-piped, disparate sets of databases to a highly integrated data environment for the enterprise;
- transition from a claim-centric orientation to a multi-view orientation that includes beneficiaries, providers, health plans, claims, drug code data, [10] clinical data, and other data as needed;
- provide uniform privacy and security controls;
- provide database scalability to meet current and expanding volumes of CMS data; and
- provide users the capability to analyze the data in place instead of relying on data extracts.

According to IDR program officials, CMS envisioned that IDR would become the single repository for the agency's data and enable data analysis within and across programs. Specifically, IDR was to establish the infrastructure for storing data for Medicare Parts A, B, and D,[11] as well as a variety of other CMS functions, such as program management, research, analytics, and business intelligence. CMS envisioned an incremental approach to incorporating data into IDR. Specifically, program plans provided to the Office of Management and Budget (OMB) by the Office of Information Services in 2006 stated that all Medicare Part D data would be incorporated into IDR by the end of that fiscal year. CMS's 2007 plans added the incorporation of Medicare Parts A and B data by the end of fiscal year 2007, and Medicaid data for 5 states by the end of fiscal year 2009, 20 states by 2010, 35 by 2011, and all 50 states by the end of fiscal year 2012.

Initial program plans and schedules also included the incorporation of additional data from legacy CMS claims-processing systems that store and process data related to the entry, correction, and adjustment of claims as they are being processed, along with detailed financial data related to paid claims. According to program officials, these data, called "shared systems" data, are needed to support the agency's plans to incorporate tools to conduct predictive analysis of claims as they are being processed, helping to prevent improper payments.[12] Shared systems data, such as check numbers and amounts related to claims that have been paid, are also needed by law enforcement agencies to help with fraud investigations.[13] CMS initially planned to include all the shared systems data in IDR by July 2008. Figure 1 shows a timeline of initial plans for incorporating data into IDR.

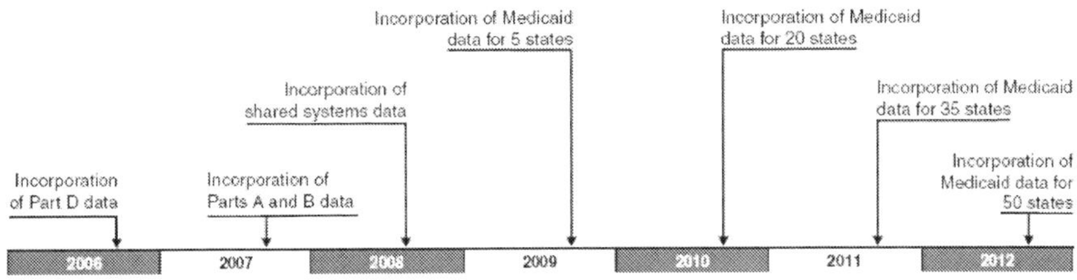

Source: GAO based on CMS data.

Figure 1. Initial Plans for Incorporating Data into IDR.

CMS's Initiative to Develop and Implement Analytical Tools for Detecting Fraud, Waste, and Abuse

In 2006, CMS's Office of Financial Management initiated the One PI program with the intention of developing and implementing a portal and software tools that would enable access to and analysis of claims, provider, and beneficiary data from a centralized source. CMS's goal for One PI was to support the needs of a broad program integrity user community, including agency program integrity personnel and contractors who analyze Medicare claims data, along with state agencies that monitor Medicaid claims. To achieve its goal, agency officials planned to implement a tool set that would provide a single source of information to enable consistent, reliable, and timely analyses and improve the agency's ability to detect fraud, waste, and abuse. These tools were to be used to gather data about beneficiaries, providers, and procedures and, combined with other data, find billing aberrancies or outliers. For example, as envisioned, an analyst could use software tools to identify potentially fraudulent trends in ambulance services. He or she could gather data about claims for ambulance services and medical treatments, and then use other software to determine associations between the two types of services. If the analyst found claims for ambulance travel costs but no corresponding claims for medical treatment, the analyst may conclude that the billings for those services were possibly fraudulent.

According to agency program planning documentation, the One PI system was to be developed incrementally to provide access to data, analytical tools, and portal functionality in three phases after an initial proof of concept phase. The proof of concept phase was reportedly begun in early 2007 and focused on integrating Medicare and Medicaid data into the portal environment. After its completion, the first development phase focused on establishing a development environment in CMS's Baltimore, Maryland, data center and, according to program officials, was completed in April 2009. The second and third phases of development were planned in January 2009 to run concurrently and to focus on the technical and analytical aspects of the project, such as building the environment to integrate the analytical tools using data retrieved from IDR, sourcing claims data from the shared systems, conducting data analyses in production, and training analysts who were intended users of the system. CMS planned to complete these two phases and implement the One PI portal and two analytical tools for use by program integrity analysts on a widespread basis by the end of fiscal year 2009.

CMS's Office of Financial Management engaged contractors to develop the system. Responsibility for and management of the One PI program moved from the Office of Financial Management to the Center for Program Integrity in 2010. Figure 2 illustrates initial plans for One PI.

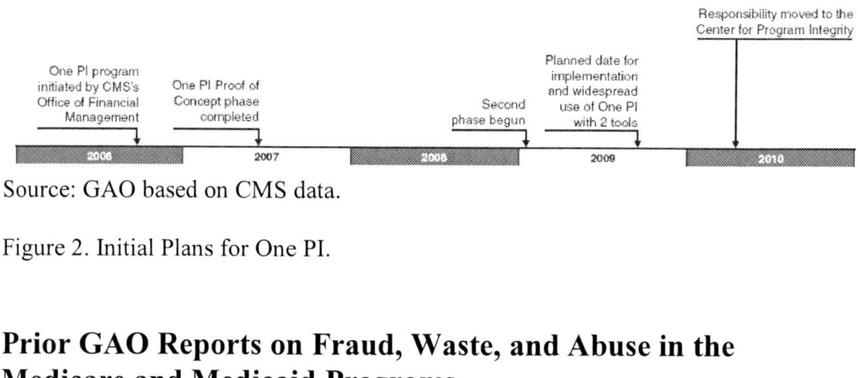

Source: GAO based on CMS data.

Figure 2. Initial Plans for One PI.

Prior GAO Reports on Fraud, Waste, and Abuse in the Medicare and Medicaid Programs

In our prior work, we have reported on CMS's efforts to detect and prevent fraudulent and improper payments in the Medicare and Medicaid programs and on its management of IT to support its mission. For example, as early as 1995, we reviewed IT systems used in the Medicare program to detect and prevent fraud and discussed the availability of other technologies to assist in combating fraudulent billing.[14] We found it was too early to fully document the cost-effectiveness of such systems, although several potential fraud cases were detected by this technology, indicating that these types of systems could provide net benefits in combating fraud. We observed that such technology could ultimately be utilized in the claims-processing environment to delay or even prevent the payment of questionable claims submitted by suspect providers.

We have also reported on weaknesses in CMS's processes for managing IT investments based upon key practices established in our Information

Technology Investment Management framework.[15] Specifically, in 2005, we evaluated CMS's capabilities for managing its internal investments, described plans the agency had for improving these capabilities, and examined the agency's process for approving and monitoring state Medicaid Management Information Systems.[16] We found that CMS had not established certain key practices for managing individual IT investments and recommended that the CMS Administrator develop and implement a plan to address the IT investment management weaknesses identified in the report. We also recommended that at a minimum, the agency should update its investment management guide to reflect current investment management processes. CMS subsequently took actions to implement each of our recommendations.

Additionally, our 2007 study of the Medicare durable medical equipment, prosthetics, orthotics, and supplies benefit found that it was vulnerable to fraud and improper payments.[17] We recommended that CMS direct its contractors to develop automated prepayment controls to identify potentially improper claims and consider adopting the most cost-effective controls of other contractors. CMS concurred with the recommendation, but has not yet implemented the prepayment controls that we recommended.

In 2009, we examined the administration of the Medicare home health benefit, which we found to leave the benefit vulnerable to fraud and improper payments.[18] We made several recommendations to the Administrator of CMS, including directing contractors to conduct post-payment medical reviews on claims submitted by home health agencies with high rates of improper billing identified through prepayment review. CMS stated it would consider two of our four recommendations—to amend regulations to expand the types of improper billing practices that are grounds for revocation of billing privileges, and to provide physicians who certify or recertify plans of care with a statement of services received by beneficiaries. CMS neither agreed nor disagreed with our other two recommendations.

Finally, in testifying on Medicare and Medicaid fraud, waste, and abuse in March 2011, we described steps that CMS could take to reduce improper payments and the agency's recent solicitation for proposals of contracts for the development and implementation of automated tools that support reviews of claims before they are paid.[19] These predictive modeling tools are intended to provide new capabilities to help prevent improper payments of Medicare claims.

IDR and One PI Have Been Developed and Implemented but without All Planned Data and Widespread Use

CMS has developed and implemented IDR and One PI for use by its program integrity analysts, but IDR does not include all the data the agency planned to have incorporated by the end of 2010, and One PI is being used by a limited number of analysts. While CMS has developed and begun using IDR, the repository does not include all the planned data, such as Medicaid and shared systems data. Program officials attribute this lack of data to insufficient planning, which did not consider unexpected obstacles or allow time for contingencies. In addition, the agency has developed and deployed One PI, but the system is being used by less than 7 percent of the intended user community and does not yet provide as many tools as planned. According to agency officials, plans to train and deploy the system to a broad community of users were disrupted when resources dedicated to these activities were redirected to address a need to improve the user training program. Further, plans and schedules for completing the remaining work have not been finalized, and CMS has not identified risks and obstacles to project schedules that may affect its ability to ensure broad use and full implementation of the systems. Until program officials finalize plans and develop reliable schedules for providing all planned data and capabilities and ensuring that One PI gains broader use throughout the program integrity community, CMS will remain at risk of experiencing additional delays in reaching widespread use and full implementation of the systems. Consequently, the agency may miss an opportunity to effectively use these IT solutions to enhance its ability to detect fraud, waste, and abuse in the Medicare and Medicaid programs.

IDR Has Been Developed and Is in Use, but Does Not Yet Include All Data Needed to Enhance Program Integrity Efforts

IDR has been in use by CMS and contractor program integrity analysts since September 2006 and currently incorporates data related to claims for reimbursement of services under Medicare Parts A, B, and D. Specifically, CMS incorporated Part D data into IDR in September 2006, as planned, and incorporated Parts A and B data by the end of fiscal year 2008. The primary source of these data is CMS's National Claims History database, from which data are extracted on a weekly basis. Other supplemental data were incorporated into IDR that are used to conduct program integrity analyses, including drug code data that are obtained from daily and weekly updates of data from CMS's Drug Data Processing System, and claims-related data about physicians that are retrieved from National Provider Index databases on a daily basis. Additionally, IDR contains data about beneficiaries that are extracted daily from the Medicare Beneficiary Database and health plan contract and benefit data that are obtained on a weekly basis from CMS's Health Plan Management Systems. According to IDR program officials with the Office of Information Services, the integration of these data into IDR established a centralized source of data previously accessed from multiple disparate system files.

CMS reported to OMB in 2010 that the agency had spent almost $48 million to establish IDR and incorporate the existing data since the program was initiated. Table 2 provides the actual costs of developing and implementing IDR for each year since fiscal year 2006, as reported to us by CMS officials.

Table 2. Reported Actual Costs of Developing and Implementing IDR, Fiscal Years 2006–2010

	2006	2007	2008	2009	2010	Total
Costs in millions	$4.7	$6.5	$10.9	$9.9	$15.6	**$47.6**

Source: CMS data.

Although the agency has been incorporating data from various data sources since 2006, IDR does not yet include all the data that were planned to be incorporated by the end of 2010 and that are needed to support enhanced program integrity initiatives. Specifically, the shared systems data that are needed to allow predictive analyses of claims are not incorporated. Without this capability, program integrity analysts are not able to access data from IDR that would help them identify and prevent payment of fraudulent claims. Additionally, IDR does not yet include the Medicaid data that are critical to analysts' ability to detect fraud, waste, and abuse in the Medicaid program.

According to IDR program officials, the shared systems data were not incorporated into IDR because, although initial program integrity requirements included the incorporation of these data by July 2008, funding for the development of the software and acquisition of the hardware needed to meet this requirement was not approved until the summer of 2010. Since then, IDR program officials have developed project plans and identified users' requirements, and plan to incorporate shared systems data by November 2011.

With respect to Medicaid data, program officials stated that the agency has not incorporated these data into IDR because the original plans and schedules for obtaining Medicaid data did not account for the lack of a mandate or funding for states to provide Medicaid data to CMS, or the variations in the types and formats of data stored in disparate state Medicaid systems. In this regard, program officials did not consider risks to the program's ability to collect the data and did not include additional time to allow for contingencies. Consequently, the IDR program officials were not able to collect the data from the states as easily as they expected and, therefore, did not complete this activity as originally planned.

In addition to the IDR program, in December 2009, CMS initiated another agencywide program intended to, among other things, identify ways to collect Medicaid data from the many disparate state systems and incorporate the data into a single data store. As envisioned by CMS, this program, the Medicaid and Children's Health Insurance Program Business Information and Solutions program, or MACBIS, is to include activities in addition to providing expedited access to current data from state Medicaid programs. For example, the MACBIS initiative is also intended to result in the development of a national system to address the needs of federal and state Medicaid partners, along with technical assistance and training for states on the use of the system. Once established, the MACBIS system data would then be incorporated into IDR and made accessible to program integrity analysts. According to program planning documentation, this enterprisewide initiative is expected to cost about $400 million through fiscal year 2016. However, plans for this program are not final, and funds for integrating Medicaid data into IDR have not yet been requested.

According to agency planning documentation, as a result of efforts to be initiated under the MACBIS program, CMS intends to incorporate Medicaid data for all 50 states into IDR by the end of fiscal year 2014. Program integrity officials stated that they plan to work with three states during 2011 to test the transfer and use of Medicaid data to help CMS determine the data that are available in those states' systems. The Center for Program Integrity is also working with Medicaid officials to establish a test environment to begin integrating state Medicaid data into IDR. Despite establishing these high-level milestones, the agency has not finalized detailed plans for incorporating the Medicaid data that include reliable schedules that identify all the necessary activities and resources for completing these efforts or the risks associated with efforts to collect and standardize data from 50 independent systems that differ in design, technology, and other characteristics dictated by state policies.

Table 3 shows the original planned dates for incorporating the various types of data and the data that were incorporated into IDR as of the end of fiscal year 2010.

Table 3. Data Incorporated into IDR as of the End of Fiscal Year 2010

Type of data	Original planned date	Actual date
Medicare Part D	January 2006	January 2006
Medicare Part B	September 2007	May 2008
Medicare Part A	September 2008	May 2008
Shared systems	July 2008	Not incorporated (planned for November 2011)
Medicaid for 5 states	September 2009	Not incorporated (planned for September 2014)
Medicaid for 20 states	September 2010	Not incorporated (planned for September 2014)
Medicaid for 35 states	September 2011	Not incorporated (planned for September 2014)
Medicaid for 50 states	September 2012	Not incorporated (planned for September 2014)

Source: GAO analysis of CMS data.

While CMS has identified target dates for incorporating the remaining data, best practices, such as those described in our cost estimation guide,[20] emphasize the importance of establishing reliable program schedules that include all activities to be performed, assign resources (labor, materials, etc.) to those activities, and identify risks and their probability and build appropriate reserve time into the schedule. However, the IDR schedule we reviewed did not identify all activities and necessary resources or include a schedule risk analysis. Such an analysis could have helped CMS identify and prepare for obstacles, such as those previously encountered in trying to incorporate Medicaid data into IDR and expected to be encountered as CMS initiates efforts to collect and standardize data from 50 state systems. Without establishing a reliable schedule for future efforts to incorporate new data sources, the agency will be at greater risk of schedule slippages, which could result in additional delays in CMS's efforts to incorporate all the data sources into IDR that are needed to support enhanced program integrity efforts.

One PI Has Been Developed but Deployed to Few Users and with Less Functionality Than Planned

According to program officials, user acceptance testing of the One PI system was completed in February 2009, and the system was deployed in September 2009 as originally planned. This initial deployment of One PI consisted of a portal that provided Web-based access to analytical tools used by program integrity analysts to retrieve and analyze data stored in IDR.

CMS reported to OMB that the agency had spent almost $114 million to develop the existing features and functionality of the One PI system by the end of fiscal year 2010. Table 4 provides information on the actual costs of developing One PI since fiscal year 2006, as reported to us by CMS officials.

Table 4. Reported Actual Costs of Developing and Implementing One PI, Fiscal Years 2006–2010

	2006	2007	2008	2009	2010	Total
Costs in millions	$.65	$15.3	$20.9	$32.9	$43.8	**$113.5**

Source: GAO analysis of CMS data.

As currently implemented, the system provides access to two analytical tools—Advantage Suite and Business Objects. Documented specifications of the One PI system described Advantage Suite as a commercial, off-theshelf decision support tool that is used to perform data analysis to, for example, detect patterns of activities that may identify or confirm suspected cases of fraud, waste, or abuse. According to program officials and the One PI users to whom we spoke, program integrity analysts use Advantage Suite to analyze claims data retrieved from IDR and create standard and custom reports that combine data about costs and quality of services, providers, and beneficiaries. The results of this level of analysis may be used to generate leads for further analysis with Business Objects, which provides users extended capabilities to perform more complex analyses of data by allowing customized queries of claims data across the three Medicare plan types. It also allows the user to create ad hoc queries and reports for nonroutine analysis.

For example, an analyst could use Advantage Suite to identify potentially fraudulent trends in ambulance services. He or she could use the tool to gather data about claims for ambulance services and medical treatments, and then use Business Objects to conduct further analysis to determine associations between the two types of services. If the analyst found claims for ambulance travel costs but no corresponding claims for medical treatment, the analyst may conclude that the billings for those services were possibly fraudulent.

Figure 3 provides a simplified view of the IDR and One PI environment as currently implemented.

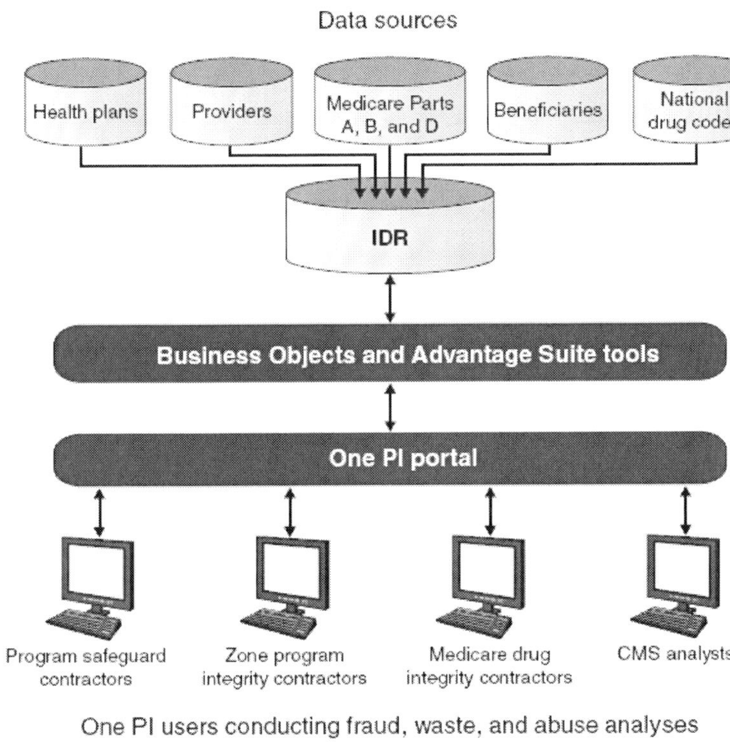

Source: GAO based on CMS data.

Figure 3. Simplified Depiction of the Current IDR and One PI Environment.

While program officials deployed the One PI portal and two analytical tools to CMS and contractor program integrity analysts, the system was not being used as widely as planned. Program planning documentation from August 2009 indicated that One PI program officials planned for 639 program integrity staff and analysts to be trained and using the system by the end of fiscal year 2010; however, CMS confirmed that by the end of October 2010 only 42 of those intended users were trained to use One PI, and 41 were actively using the portal and tools. These users represent less than 7 percent of the original intended users. Of these, 31 were contractors and 10 were CMS staff who performed analyses of claims to detect potential cases of fraud, waste, and abuse. Table 5 describes the analysts planned to be and actually using One PI at the end of fiscal year 2010.[21]

Table 5. Planned and Actual Users of One PI as of October 2010

Type of user	Planned by end of FY 2010	Actual
CMS program integrity staff	100	10
CMS program integrity contractors	159	31
Medicaid states and Medi-Medi program staff	130	0
HHS OIG staff and law enforcement	250	0
Total	639	41

Source: GAO analysis of CMS information.

According to One PI program officials, the system was not being used by the intended number of program integrity analysts because the office had not trained a sufficient number of analysts to use the system. Similarly, although CMS contractually requires Medicare program integrity contractors to use the system, officials stated that they could not enforce this requirement because they also had not trained enough of their program integrity contractors.

Although One PI program plans emphasized the importance of effective training and communications, program officials responsible for implementing the system acknowledged that their initial training plans and efforts were insufficient. According to the officials, they initially provided training for the all the components of the system—the portal, tools, and use of IDR data—in a 3-and-a-half-day course. However, they realized that the trainees did not effectively use One PI after completing the training. Consequently, program officials initiated activities and redirected resources to redesign the One PI training plan in April 2010, and began to implement the new training program in July of that year. The redesigned program includes courses on each of the system components and allows trainees to use the components to reinforce learning before taking additional courses. For example, the redesigned plan includes a One PI portal overview and data training webinars that users must complete before attending instructor-led training on Advantage Suite and Business Objects. The new plans also incorporate the use of "data coaches" who provide hands-on help to analysts, such as assistance with designing queries. Additionally, the plans require users to complete surveys to evaluate the quality of the training and their ability to use the tools after they complete each course.

As program officials took the initiative and time to redesign the training program, this effort caused delays in CMS's plans to train the intended number of users. Since the new training program was implemented, the number of users has not yet significantly increased, but the number of contractor analysts requesting training has increased. Specifically, One PI officials told us that 62 individuals had signed up to be trained in 2011, and that the number of training classes for One PI was increased from two to four per month. The officials also stated that they planned to reach out to and train more contractors and staff from the HHS OIG and the Department of Justice to promote One PI. They anticipated that 12 inspectors general and 12 law enforcement officials would be trained and using One PI by the end of May 2011.

Nonetheless, while these activities indicate some progress toward increasing the number of One PI users, the number of users expected to be trained and to begin using the system represents a small fraction of the population of 639 intended users. Additionally, One PI program officials had not yet made detailed plans and developed schedules for completing training of all the intended users. Further, although program officials had scheduled more training classes, they have not established deadlines for contractor analysts to attend training so that they are able to fulfill the contractual requirement to use One PI. Unless the agency takes more aggressive steps to ensure that its program integrity community is trained, it will not be able to require the use of the system by its contractors, and the use of One PI may remain limited to a much smaller group of users than the agency intended. As a result, CMS will continue to face obstacles in its efforts to deploy One PI to the intended number of program integrity users as the agency continues to develop and implement additional features and functionalities in the system.

Additionally, although efforts to develop and implement One PI were initiated in 2006 and the Advantage Suite and Business Objects tools are fully developed, implemented, and in use, the One PI system does not yet include additional analytical functionality that CMS initially planned to implement by the end of 2010. Program documentation for the system includes plans for future phases of One PI development to incrementally add new analytical tools, additional sources of data, and expanded portal functionality, such as enhanced communications support, and specifically included the integration of a third tool by the end of fiscal year 2010. However, program officials have not yet identified users' needs for functionality that could be provided by another tool, such as the capability to access and analyze more data from IDR than the current implementation of the system provides. According to program officials, they intend to determine users' needs for additional functionality when the system becomes more widely used by agency and contractor analysts who are able to identify deficiencies and define additional features and functionality needed to improve its effectiveness.

Additionally, as with IDR, in developing the One PI schedule estimate that was provided to OMB in 2010, program officials did not complete a risk assessment for the schedule that identified potential obstacles to the program. As a result, they lacked information needed to plan for additional time to address contingencies when obstacles arose. As the program office makes plans for deploying the system to the wide community of program integrity analysts and implementing additional tools, it is crucial that officials identify potential obstacles to the schedules and the risks they may introduce to the completion of related activities. For example, an analysis that identified the risk that resources would need to be redirected to other elevated priorities, such as user training, could have informed managers of the need to include additional time and resources in the schedule to help keep the development and deployment of One PI on track. Unless program officials complete a risk assessment of schedules for ongoing and future activities, CMS faces risks of perpetuating delays in establishing widespread use of One PI and achieving full implementation of the system for increased rates of fraud, waste, and abuse detection.

CMS Is Not Yet Positioned to Fully Meet Goals and Objectives for Detecting Fraud, Waste, and Abuse through the Use of IDR and One PI

Our prior work emphasized agencies' need to ensure that IT investments actually produce improvements in mission performance.[22] As we have reported, agencies should forecast expected benefits and then measure actual financial benefits accrued through the implementation of IT programs. Further, OMB requires agencies to report progress against performance measures and targets for meeting them that reflect the goals and objectives of the programs. To do this, performance measures should be outcome-based, developed with stakeholder input, and monitored and compared to planned results.[23] Additionally, industry experts describe the need for performance measures to be developed with stakeholders' input early in a project's planning process to provide a central management and planning tool and to monitor the performance of the project against plans and stakeholders' needs.[24]

While CMS has made progress toward meeting the programs' goals of providing a centralized data repository and enhanced analytical capabilities for program integrity efforts, the current implementation of IDR and One PI does not position the agency to identify, measure, and track financial benefits realized from reductions in improper payments as a result of the implementation of either system. Additionally, program officials have not developed and tracked outcome-based performance measures to help ensure that efforts to implement One PI and IDR meet the agency's goals and objectives for improving the results of its program integrity initiatives. For example, outcome-based measures for the programs would indicate improvements to the agency's ability to recover funds lost because of improper payments of fraudulent claims. Until CMS is better positioned to identify and measure financial benefits and outcome-based performance measures to help gauge progress toward meeting program integrity goals, it cannot be assured that the systems will contribute to improvements in CMS's ability to detect fraud, waste, and abuse in the Medicare and Medicaid programs, and prevent or recover billions of dollars lost to improper payments of claims.

CMS Has Made Limited Progress toward Meeting Program Integrity Goals and Objectives through the Use of IDR

As stated in program planning documentation, IDR's overall goal is to integrate Medicare and Medicaid data so that CMS and its partners may access the data from a single source. Specifically, the implementation of IDR was expected to result in financial benefits associated with the program's goal to transition from a data environment of stove-piped, disparate databases and systems to an integrated data environment.

Officials with the Office of Information Services stated that they developed estimates of financial benefits expected to be realized through the use of IDR. In 2006, program officials projected financial benefits from IDR of $152 million at an estimated cost of $82 million, or a net benefit of about $70 million. In 2007 these officials revised their projection of total financial benefits to $187 million based on their estimates of the amount of improper payments they expected to be recovered as a result of analyzing data provided by IDR. The resulting net benefit expected from implementing IDR was estimated to be $97 million in 2010 due to changes in program cost estimates.

Table 6 includes CMS's estimated financial benefits, costs, and net benefits reported to OMB for the lifecycle of the program from fiscal year 2006 to 2010.[25]

Table 6. Reported Estimated and Actual Costs and Benefits of IDR

Dollars in millions						
Projected program benefits and costs	**2006 lifecycle estimate (FY 2005-2012)[a]**	**2007 lifecycle estimate (FY 2005-2013)**	**2008 lifecycle estimate (FY 2005-2015)**	**2009 lifecycle estimate (FY 2005-2016)**	**2010 lifecycle estimate (FY 2005-2018)**	**Actual costs and benefits (FY 2006-2010)**
Benefits	152	187	187[b]	187[b]	187[b]	Not known
Costs	82	86	92	116	90	44
Net benefit	70	101	95	71	97	Not known

Source: GAO based on CMS data.

[a] initial estimates include planning costs from FY 2005.

[b] Because the agency has not updated the benefits estimate, we carried this figure forward.

However, as of March 2011, program officials had not identified actual financial benefits of implementing IDR based on the recovery of improper payments. In our discussions with the Office of Information Services, program officials stated they determined that deploying IDR led to the avoidance of IT costs as a result of the retirement of several legacy systems attributable to the implementation of IDR. However, they had not quantified these or any other financial benefits. Until officials measure and track financial benefits related to program goals, CMS officials cannot be assured that the use of the system is helping the agency prevent or recover funds lost as a result of improper payments of Medicare and Medicaid claims.

Additionally, while program officials defined and reported to OMB performance targets for IDR related to some of the program's goals, they do not reflect its goal to provide a single source of Medicare and Medicaid data for program integrity efforts. Although progress made to date in implementing IDR supports the program's goals to transition CMS to an integrated data environment, program officials have not defined and reported to OMB performance measures to gauge the extent to which the program is meeting this goal. Specifically, IDR officials defined performance measures for technical indicators, such as incorporating Medicare data into the repository, making the data available for analysis, and reducing the number of databases

CMS must support, but they have not defined measures and targets that reflect the extent to which all the data needed to support program integrity initiatives are incorporated into a single source, including the Medicaid and shared systems data which have not yet been incorporated into IDR. Further, the IDR performance measures do not reflect indicators that may lead to the program's ability to achieve the financial benefits defined by the agency's program integrity initiatives.

In discussing this matter, IDR officials stated that the performance measures for the program are only intended to track progress toward implementing technical capabilities of the system, such as the amount of data from specific sources incorporated into the repository and made available through software tools to analysts. They do not define performance indicators, measures, and targets for incorporating data from future sources of data until plans are made and funds are provided by the agency's business offices to begin activities to implement new functionalities into IDR. IDR program officials also stated that they do not define or track business-related performance indicators for achieving specific program integrity goals; rather, they depend upon business owners to measure and track these indicators based upon the use of IDR data to achieve business goals. However, without performance measures that reflect business owners' and other stakeholders' needs for the program to deliver a single source of all Medicare and Medicaid data needed to conduct analyses, and lacking measures that reflect the success of the program toward achieving financial benefits projected for program integrity initiatives, program officials lack key management information needed to ensure that the data and infrastructure components provided by IDR enhance CMS's ability to meet its program integrity goals and objectives. Without this assurance, the effectiveness of the system's capability to increase rates of fraud, waste, and abuse detection and, consequently, decrease the amount of money lost to improper payments of claims will remain unknown.

CMS Is Not Yet Positioned to Demonstrate Improvements in Its Ability to Meet Goals and Objectives for Detecting Fraud, Waste, and Abuse through the Use of One PI

The Center for Program Integrity's overall goal for One PI was to provide robust tools for accessing a single source of information to enable consistent, reliable, and timely analyses to improve the agency's ability to detect fraud, waste, and abuse. Achieving this goal was intended to result in the recovery of significant funds lost each year from improper payments of Medicare and Medicaid claims. In September 2007, program officials projected financial benefits from implementing One PI—nearly $13 billion over the 10-year lifecycle of the project. According to program officials, these benefits were expected to accrue from the recovery of improper payments of Medicare and Medicaid claims and reduced program integrity contractor expenditures for supporting IT required to maintain separate databases.

In September 2007, One PI officials projected and reported to OMB benefits of nearly $13 billion. They subsequently revised this estimate to approximately $21 billion. Program officials told us that increases in the projected financial benefits were made based on assumptions that accelerated plans to integrate Medicare and Medicaid data into a central data repository would enable One PI users to identify increasing numbers of improper payments sooner than previously estimated, thus allowing the agency to recover more funds lost due to payment errors. Table 7 provides data CMS reported to OMB on estimated benefits and costs, actual costs as of the end of fiscal year 2010, and net benefits projected to be realized as a result of implementing One PI from fiscal year 2007 through 2010.

Table 7. Reported Estimated and Actual Costs and Benefits of One PI

Dollars in millions					
Projected program benefits and costs	**2007 lifecycle estimate (FY 2006-2013)[a]**	**2008 lifecycle estimate (FY 2006-2014)**	**2009 lifecycle estimate (FY 2006-2015)**	**2010 lifecycle estimate (FY 2006-2015)**	**Actual costs and benefits (FY 2006-2010)**
Benefit	$12,722	$15,785[b]	$21,358[b]	$21,358[b]	Not known
Costs	199	233	275	255	114
Net benefit	12,523	15, 552	21,083	21,103	Not known

Source: GAO analysis of CMS data.

[a]One PI officials initially projected system benefits from fiscal year 2008 through fiscal year 2013. [b]Because the agency has not updated the benefits estimate, we carried this figure forward.

However, the current implementation of One PI has not yet produced outcomes that position the agency to identify or measure financial benefits. Therefore, the net financial benefit of developing and implementing One PI remains unknown. Center for Program Integrity officials stated that at the end of fiscal year 2010—over a year after deploying One PI—it was too early to determine whether the program has provided any financial benefits because, since the program had not met its goal for widespread use of One PI, there were not enough data available to quantify financial benefits attributable to the use of the system. These officials anticipated that as the user community is expanded, they will be able to begin to identify and measure financial and other benefits of using the system. However, the officials also indicated that they had not yet defined mechanisms for determining the amount of money recovered as a result of detecting improper payments through the use of One PI. As with IDR, until the agency quantifies and tracks the progress it is making in delivering benefits intended to be realized through widespread use of One PI, CMS officials cannot be assured of the cost-effectiveness of implementing One PI to help the agency meet its goal to enable consistent, reliable, and timely analyses of data to improve the agency's ability to detect fraud, waste, and abuse.

Additionally, in discussion groups held with active One PI users, program integrity analysts identified several issues that confirmed the agency's limited progress toward meeting the goals of the program. For example, while several users told us that the One PI system can support their work, they recognized limited progress toward the establishment of a single source of information and analysis tools for all fraud, waste, and abuse activities. Further, One PI users stated that the system enabled analysts to access national data not otherwise accessible to them and supported analysis across different Medicare programs. They also noted that the tools offered by One PT provided more functionality than other tools they use. However, of the analysts in the discussion groups, most did not use One PT as their only source of information and analysis for detecting improper payments. Rather, to help conduct their work, they relied on other analysis tools provided by CMS or their companies, along with data from CMS claims processing contractors or from private databases created by other contractors.

One PT users in the discussion groups also told us that they use other tools because they are more familiar with those tools. Additionally, they stated that other databases sometimes provide data that are not currently accessible through One PT and TDR, such as demographic data about providers. Program integrity analysts further stated that they only use One PT as a cross-check of data and analysis from their own systems because they are not yet convinced that One PT can be used as a replacement for or adjunct to those data sources and tools.

Further, CMS officials have not developed quantifiable measures for meeting the program's goals. CMS officials defined and reported to OMB performance measures and targets toward meeting the program's goals for enabling timely analyses of data to detect cases of fraud, waste, and abuse, but have not yet been able to quantify measures for these indicators. For example, performance measures and targets for One PT include increases in the detection of improper payments for Medicare Parts A and B claims. However, according to program integrity officials, measures had not yet been quantified because they had not yet identified ways to determine the extent to which increases in the detection of errors could be attributed to the use of One PT. Additionally, the limited use of the system has not generated enough data to quantify the amount of funds recovered from improper payments. Moreover, measures of One PT's program performance do not accurately reflect the current state of the program. Specifically, indicators to be measured for the program include the number of states using One PT (for Medicaid integrity purposes) and decreases in the Medicaid payment error rate, but One PT does not have access to those data because they are not yet incorporated into TDR. Therefore, these performance indicators are not relevant to the current implementation of the system.

Finally, CMS officials did not consult external system users (e.g., program integrity contractors) in developing measures of One PI's effectiveness. According to industry experts, [26] developing performance measures with stakeholder input early in the planning process can provide a mechanism for gauging the effectiveness of outcomes toward meeting business needs and achieving program goals as a program progresses. However, CMS officials did not consult external users of the system about how they would measure its effectiveness. According to program officials, program integrity stakeholders within CMS were involved in the development of the performance measures; however, external users of the system were not asked to provide input when it may have been used to establish an effective performance tracking tool, such as when defining ways to determine whether One PI meets stakeholders' needs. For example, program officials told us that they intend to determine user satisfaction, a performance measure reported to OMB, by conducting surveys at the end of training sessions. However, these surveys were conducted before the analysts actually used the system in their work and were focused on satisfaction with the training itself. In this case, involvement of external stakeholders when defining the measure could have led to more effective ways to determine user satisfaction, such as surveying analysts based on their experiences resulting from the use of One PI after a certain period of time defined by stakeholders.

Until they define measurable performance indicators and targets that reflect the goals and objectives of CMS's program integrity initiatives, agency officials will continue to lack the information needed to ensure that the implementation of One PI helps improve the agency's ability to identify improper payments and to detect cases of fraud, waste, and abuse. Additionally, when lacking stakeholders' input into the process for determining measures of successful performance, One PI program officials may miss an opportunity to obtain information needed to define meaningful measures that reflect the success of the program toward meeting users' and the agency's needs. Because it lacks meaningful outcome-based performance measures and effective methods for tracking progress toward meeting performance targets, CMS does not have the information needed to ensure that the system is useful to the extent that benefits realized from the implementation of One PI help the agency meet program integrity goals.

CONCLUSION

IDR and One PI program officials have made progress in developing and implementing IDR and One PI to support CMS's program integrity initiatives, but the systems do not yet provide all the data and functionality initially planned. Additionally, CMS program integrity officials have not yet taken appropriate actions to ensure the use of IDR and One PI on a widespread basis for program integrity purposes. Further, program officials have not defined plans and reliable schedules for incorporating the additional data into IDR that are needed to support its program integrity goals. Until the agency takes these steps, it cannot ensure that ongoing development, implementation, and deployment efforts will provide the data and technical capabilities needed to improve program integrity analysts' capabilities for detecting potential cases of fraud, waste, and abuse.

Furthermore, because the systems are not being used as planned, CMS program integrity officials are not yet in a position to determine the extent to which the systems are providing financial benefits or supporting the agency's initiatives to meet its program integrity goals and objectives. Until it does so, CMS officials will lack the means to determine whether the use of the systems contributes to the agency's goal of reducing the number and amounts of improper payments made as a result of fraudulent, wasteful, or abusive claims for Medicare and Medicaid services. Furthermore, the contribution of IDR and One PI to the agency's efforts to save billions of dollars each year attributable to improper payments made due to fraud, waste, and abuse in the Medicare and Medicaid programs will remain unknown.

Recommendations for Executive Action

To help ensure that the development and implementation of IDR and One PI are successful in helping the agency meet the goals and objectives of its program integrity initiatives, we are recommending that the Administrator of CMS take the following seven actions:

- finalize plans and develop schedules for incorporating additional data into IDR that identify all resources and activities needed to complete tasks and that consider risks and obstacles to the IDR program;
- implement and manage plans for incorporating data in IDR to meet schedule milestones;
- establish plans and reliable schedules for training all program integrity analysts intended to use One PI;
- establish and communicate deadlines for program integrity contractors to complete training and use One PI in their work;
- conduct training in accordance with plans and established deadlines to ensure schedules are met and program integrity contractors are trained and able to meet requirements for using One PI;
- define any measurable financial benefits expected from the implementation of IDR and One PI; and
- with stakeholder input, establish measurable, outcome-based performance measures for IDR and One PI that gauge progress toward meeting program goals.

Agency Comments and Our Evaluation

In written comments on a draft of this chapter, CMS stated that it concurred with all of our recommendations and identified steps agency officials were taking to implement them.

Among these were actions to further refine training plans to better ensure that program integrity contractors are trained and able to meet requirements to use One PI, along with efforts to define measurable financial benefits expected from augmenting the data in IDR.

If these and other identified actions are implemented in accordance with our recommendations, CMS will be better positioned to meet the goals and objectives of its program integrity initiatives. The agency also provided technical comments, which were incorporated as appropriate.

Valerie C. Melvin
Director,
Information Management and Human Capital Issues

APPENDIX I: OBJECTIVES, SCOPE, AND METHODOLOGY

The objectives of our review were to (1) assess the extent to which the Centers for Medicare and Medicaid Services (CMS) has developed and implemented the Integrated Data Repository (IDR) and One Program Integrity (One PI) systems and (2) determine the agency's progress toward achieving defined goals and objectives for using the systems to help detect fraud, waste, and abuse in the Medicare and Medicaid programs.

To assess the extent to which IDR and One PI have been developed and implemented, we collected and analyzed agency documentation that described planning and management activities. Specifically, we assessed project management plans and artifacts that described the status of the systems, such as program management review briefings to technical review boards, and memoranda approving continued development and implementation of the systems at key decision points in the systems' lifecycles. We observed the operation of CMS's data center where IDR is installed and viewed a demonstration of the One PI portal and analytical tools. We also discussed with officials from CMS's Office of Information Services and Center for Program Integrity plans for and progress made toward developing and implementing the systems. We focused our analysis on the extent to which the development and implementation of IDR and One PI met system and business requirements and plans for deploying the systems to CMS's program integrity analysts.

To assess the agency's processes for defining system requirements, we reviewed IDR and One PI requirements management plans, system requirements, and documentation that traces requirements to functionality provided by the systems at different stages of implementation. Program documents we reviewed include the 2007 IDR Medicare Program Integrity Requirements, the 2006 One PI Startup Findings Draft, the 2010 One PI Requirements Management Plan, and detailed software requirements specifications for One PI. In addition, we discussed with IDR and One PI program officials their requirements development and management processes and procedures. We then assessed the department's current approach to requirements development and management against best practices identified in the Software Engineering Institute's Capability Maturity Model Integration.

To assess schedule estimates of the IDR and One PI programs, we used criteria defined in GAO's cost estimating and assessment guide to determine the extent to which relevant schedules were prepared in accordance with best practices that are fundamental to estimating reliable schedules. We identified information reported to the Office of Management and Budget (OMB) by CMS in fiscal year 2010 that defined program schedule estimates for the remaining lifecycles of the programs through 2016. We collected and analyzed program documentation that supported these estimates, such as work breakdown structures and staffing estimates.

To assess each program's schedule estimates, we rated the IDR and One PI program management offices' implementation of nine scheduling best practices defined in our guidance. Based on these criteria, we analyzed the One PI integrated master schedule and the IDR validation, along with supporting documentation, and used commercially available software tools to assess the schedules. Specifically, we determined whether each schedule was developed by identifying and including critical elements of reliable scheduling best practices, such as identifying all resources needed to conduct activities, and whether risk assessment and contingency plans had been conducted for the schedules.

We shared our guidance, the criteria against which we evaluated the program's schedule estimates, as well as our preliminary findings with program officials. We then discussed our preliminary assessment results with the program management officials. When warranted, we updated our analyses based on the agency response and additional documentation provided to us. We also analyzed changes to the program schedules over time.

To determine the reliability of the data used to assess schedule estimates, we used a scheduling analysis software tool that identified missing logic and constraints, and checked for specific problems that could hinder the schedule's ability to dynamically respond to changes. We examined the schedule data to identify any open-ended activities (i.e., activities with no predecessor or successors), and searched for activities with poor logic, such as activities with constraints that keep the schedule rigid (e.g., start no earlier than, finish no later than, etc.). We found the data sufficiently reliable for the purposes of this review.

To determine the number of system end users for One PI, we identified the universe of analysts trained to use One PI by examining documentation provided by CMS. Specifically, we obtained a list of trained users from the Center for Program Integrity. From that list, we selected program integrity analysts whom CMS identified as using the system to conduct analyses of IDR data to identify potential cases of fraud, waste, and abuse. We then compared this selection of analysts to data generated by the One PI system that recorded user login data from January 3, 2010, through October 16, 2010, to identify the current population of One PI users. Through this analysis, we identified 41 trained program integrity analysts who had used the system during the designated time period, including 8 Medicare drug integrity contractors, 23 zone program integrity and program safeguard contractors, and 10 CMS program integrity analysts.

To ensure that the data that we used to identify One PI users were reliable, we held discussions with CMS officials who were knowledgeable of the user community and mechanisms for accessing the system. We discussed with them the list of trained end users and the computer-generated login information provided by the system. We also discussed the reliability of the computer-generated system login information. Specifically, agency officials confirmed that the data reported by the system were complete and accurate and that the method we used to identify active users—an analysis of system login data—was valid.

To determine the extent to which the IDR and One PI programs have achieved defined goals and objectives for using the systems to help detect fraud, waste, and abuse, we collected CMS's analyses of projected costs and benefits for IDR and One PI. We also collected and assessed data reported on the costs and benefits realized through the current implementation of the systems. To do so, we compared (1) actual costs and benefits attributed to each system through fiscal year 2010 and (2) current estimated total lifecycle costs and benefits for each system. We calculated the expected net benefit by subtracting estimated and actual system costs from estimated and actual system benefits for each system. To understand how costs and benefits for each system were derived, we met with officials from the Office of Information Services and from the Center for Program Integrity and discussed CMS's processes for estimating and tracking costs and benefits of both IDR and One PI. We also obtained from agency officials documentation about and descriptions of qualitative benefits provided by both systems. Additionally, we reviewed planning documents that described the goals and objectives of both programs, along with other documentation that described actions taken to address program goals and objectives. We reviewed and assessed supporting documentation for the measures, which the agency reported to OMB as having been met.

To determine if CMS's approach to developing performance measures for IDR and One PI was consistent with federal guidance, we examined documents describing CMS's approach and held discussions with program officials about practices they followed when defining performance measures and targets. We compared program officials' practices to guidance defined by OMB. We also compared the performance measures defined for the two programs to CMS's goals and objectives for program integrity initiatives to determine if the IDR and One PI measures supported intended outcomes of agencywide efforts to better detect fraud, waste, and abuse. We supplemented our documentation review with interviews of officials from the Center for Program Integrity and the Office of Information Services to obtain additional information about the development of current and future performance measures for IDR and One PI. During our interviews, we discussed performance measures and strategic goals and initiatives for One PI and IDR, and the extent to which the agency involved internal and external stakeholders in the development of performance measures.

To obtain information about the extent to which One PI has been deployed and is being used by a broad community of program integrity analysts to meet CMS's goals and objectives, we invited the 41 users we identified in addressing the first objective of this engagement to participate in facilitated discussions about the data and tools needed to support fraud, waste, and abuse detection. Thirty-two of those 41 users attended the discussion group meetings. During those meetings, we discussed the following topics: usage of One PI tools and data from IDR, comparison and contrasting of One PI and IDR with other tools and data sets, and benefits and challenges of using One PI and IDR for detecting fraud, waste, and abuse. We also discussed users' needs for analytical tools and data and for systems training. After those discussions, we sent written questions to all 32 discussion group participants to obtain more detailed information about their use of analytical tools and data sources. Thirty-one participants responded and provided additional supplementary information about their use of One PI and IDR.

For each of the objectives, we assessed the reliability of the data we analyzed through interviews with agency officials knowledgeable of the user community and training program, mechanisms for accessing the systems, and the methods for tracking and reporting costs and schedules of the IDR and One

PI programs. We found the data sufficiently reliable for the purposes of this review.

We conducted this performance audit from June 2010 through June 2011 in accordance with generally accepted government auditing standards. Those standards require that we plan and perform the audit to obtain sufficient, appropriate evidence to provide a reasonable basis for our findings and conclusions based on our audit objectives. We believe that the evidence obtained provides a reasonable basis for our findings and conclusions based on our audit objectives.

End Notes

[1] GAO, *High-Risk Series: An Update,* GAO-11-278 (Washington, D.C.: February 2011).

[2] The One PI portal is a Web-based user interface that enables a single login through centralized, role-based access to the system.

[3] The Software Engineering Institute is a federally funded research and development center that conducts software engineering research in areas such as acquisition and process improvement and performance measurement. The institute is based at Carnegie Mellon University and is sponsored by the Department of Defense's Under Secretary for Acquisition, Technology, and Logistics.

[4] Social Security Act §§ 1903 (codified at 42 U.S.C. § 1396b), 1905 (codified at 42 U.S.C. § 1396d).

[5] HIPAA established the Medicare Integrity Program and codified the program integrity activities previously known as "payment safeguards." Pub. L. No. 104-191, § 202, 110 Stat. 1936, 1996, SSA §1893 (codified at 42 U.S.C. § 1395ddd).

[6] CMS is phasing out its use of program safeguard contractors, the predecessors to zone program integrity contractors. In implementing a 2003 statute, CMS began to consolidate all program integrity functions for seven geographically based zones under one type of contractor to replace the program safeguard structure, which organized contractor functions by program types. This effort is ongoing. Currently, both types of contractors perform program integrity functions for the agency.

[7] The Medi-Medi program was established in 2001 and designed to identify improper billing and utilization patterns by matching Medicare and Medicaid claims information on providers and beneficiaries to reduce fraudulent schemes that cross program boundaries. The Social Security Act provides funds for CMS to contract with third parties to identify program vulnerabilities in Medicare and Medicaid through examining billing and payment abnormalities. The funds also can be used in connection with the Medi-Medi program for two other purposes: (1) coordinating actions by CMS, the states, the Attorney General, and the HHS Office of the Inspector General to protect Medicaid and Medicare expenditures, and (2) increasing the effectiveness and efficiency of both Medicare and Medicaid through cost avoidance, savings, and recouping fraudulent, wasteful, or abusive expenditures. The program is implemented in 10 states.

[8] Pub. L. No. 109-171, § 6034, 120 Stat. 4, 74-78 (2006).

[9] Department of Health and Human Services, Office of the Inspector General, *Medicare's Program Safeguard Contractors: Activities to Detect and Deter Fraud and Abuse,* OEI-03-06-00010 (Washington, D.C., July 2007).

[10] To meet requirements of the Federal Food, Drug, and Cosmetic Act, 21 U.S.C. § 360, establishments that make or process drugs identify and report drugs for human use to HHS's Food and Drug Administration by a unique, three-segment number, called the National Drug Code.

[11] Medicare Advantage plans are not currently required to report Part C claims data to CMS and, while CMS does not yet collect these data, it plans to do so in the future. Additionally, CMS intends to incorporate data about Part C patient encounters and episodes of care into IDR but has not yet begun to plan this activity.

[12] CMS was recently required by the Small Business Jobs Act of 2010 and received funding to add predictive modeling and other analytic techniques—known as predictive analytic technologies—both to identify and to prevent improper payments under the Medicare fee-for-service. Through such analysis, unusual or suspicious patterns or abnormalities could be identified and used to prioritize additional review of suspicious transactions before payment is made.

[13] In addition to the data that CMS plans to incorporate into IDR, recent legislation mandates the inclusion of other data to support improvements in outcomes of program integrity efforts. Specifically, the Patient Protection and Affordable Care Act requires HHS to expand IDR to include claims and payment data from the Departments of Veterans Affairs and Defense, the Indian Health Service, and the Social Security Administration. According to HHS's OIG, the intention of this requirement of the act is to foster data-matching agreements among CMS and these agencies to make it easier to detect fraud, waste, and abuse. However, IDR program officials stated that CMS has not yet developed plans and established schedules for including the data required to meet this mandate.

[14] GAO, *Medicare: Antifraud Technology Offers Significant Opportunity to Reduce Health Care Fraud*, GAO/AIMD-95-77 (Washington, D.C.: Aug. 11, 1995).

[15] GAO, *Information Technology: Centers for Medicare & Medicaid Services Needs to Establish Critical Investment Management Capabilities*, GAO-06-12 (Washington, D.C.: Oct. 28, 2005). The Information Technology Investment Management framework is a maturity model developed by GAO that comprises five progressive stages of maturity that an agency can achieve in its investment management capabilities.

[16] The Medicaid Management Information System is the primary claims processing and information retrieval system that CMS requires states to use in their Medicaid programs.

[17] GAO, *Medicare: Improvements Needed to Address Improper Payments for Medical Equipment and Supplies,* GAO-07-59 (Washington, D.C.: Jan. 31, 2007).

[18] GAO, *Medicare: Improvements Needed to Address Improper Payments in Home Health,* GAO-09-185 (Washington, D.C.: Feb. 27, 2009).

[19] GAO, *Medicare and Medicaid Fraud, Waste, and Abuse: Effective Implementation of Recent Laws and Agency Actions Could Help Reduce Improper Payments*, GAO-11-409T (Washington, D.C.: Mar. 9, 2011).

[20] GAO, *GAO Cost Estimating and Assessment Guide: Best Practices for Developing and Managing Capital Program Costs*, GAO-09-3SP (Washington, D.C.: March 2009).

[21] One PI program officials told us in April 2011 that about 60 more program integrity analysts had begun to use the system. The scope, methodology, and time frame of our study limited our analysis to data based on information available from CMS through October 2010. Therefore, we did not validate program officials' April estimate.

[22] GAO, *Secure Border Initiative: DHS Needs to Reconsider Its Proposed Investment in Key Technology Program*, GAO-10-340 (Washington, D.C.: May 5, 2010) and *DOD Business Systems Modernization: Planned Investment in Navy Program to Create Cashless Shipboard Environment Needs to be Justified and Better Managed*, GAO-08-922 (Washington, D.C.: Sept. 8, 2008).

[23] OMB, *Guide to the Performance Assessment Rating Tool.*

[24] Thomas Wettstein and Peter Kueng, *A Maturity Model for Performance Measurement Systems,* and Karen J. Richter, Ph.D., Institute for Defense Analyses, CMMI®for Acquisition (CMMI-ACQ) Primer, Version 1.2.

[25] The number of lifecycle years reported for an IT project is defined by OMB. Agencies report accordingly.

[26] Thomas Wettstein and Peter Kueng, *A Maturity Model for Performance Measurement Systems.*

In: Fraud Detection and Deterrence … ISBN: 978-1-62417-658-6
Editor: Anton Ferilli

Chapter 2

BACKGROUND MEMO FOR THE HEARING ON "MEDICARE CONTRACTORS' EFFORTS TO FIGHT FRAUD: MOVING BEYOND 'PAY AND CHASE'"*

House Committee on Energy and Commerce, Subcommittee on Oversight and Investigations

TO:	Members, Subcommittee on Oversight and Investigations
FROM:	Subcommittee on Oversight and Investigations Staff
RE:	Hearing on "Medicare Contractors' Efforts to Fight Fraud – Moving Beyond 'Pay and Chase'"

On Friday, June 8, 2012, at 9:30 a.m. in room 2123 of the Rayburn House Office Building, the Subcommittee on Oversight and Investigations will hold a hearing entitled "Medicare Contractors' Efforts to Fight Fraud – Moving Beyond 'Pay and Chase'."

To combat fraud, the U.S. Department of Health and Human Services (HHS), Centers for Medicare and Medicaid Services (CMS) contracts with a number of private entities to conduct program integrity activities such as preventing, detecting, and recovering fraudulent Medicare payments. The

* This is an edited, reformatted and augmented version of a Background Memo given on June 8, 2012 before the House Committee on Energy and Commerce, Subcommittee on Oversight and Investigations.

purpose of the hearing is to examine CMS oversight of its Medicare contractors and to identify ways to improve the contractors' effectiveness at preventing and combating fraud.

I. WITNESSES

One panel of witnesses will testify at the hearing:
Mr. Robert A. Vito
Regional Inspector General, Office of Evaluations and Inspections
Office of Inspector General
U.S. Department of Health and Human Services

Ms. Kathleen M. King
Director, Health Care
U.S. Government Accountability Office

Mr. Ted Doolittle
Deputy Director, Center for Program Integrity
Centers for Medicare and Medicaid Services
U.S. Department of Health and Human Services

II. BACKGROUND

Since 1990, the Government Accountability Office (GAO) has designated Medicare as a Federal program at high risk for fraud and abuse. Although estimates of the dollar amount lost to health care fraud can vary greatly, analysts agree that tens of billions of dollars are lost every year.[1] The most common types of fraud include: billing for services that were not performed or billing for a higher level of service than was performed; billing for equipment that was not delivered; the use of another individual's Medicare card to obtain care, supplies, or equipment; and billing for home medical equipment after it was returned. While anti-fraud efforts have rightfully shifted towards prevention, Medicare is required to process and pay most claims within thirty days, making it hard to conduct thorough prepayment reviews and completely pivot away from a "pay and chase" approach. Regardless of the approach employed, Medicare contractors are often the first and last line of defense against fraud and abuse.

As the agency responsible for administering Medicare, CMS contracts with a number of private entities to conduct various anti-fraud activities. In April 2010, CMS consolidated responsibility for administering and monitoring "program integrity" efforts, including contractor oversight, under a newly created organizational entity, the Center for Program Integrity (CPI). CMS identified CPI's overarching mission to be "protecting the Trust Funds and other public resources against losses from fraud and other improper payments and to improve the integrity of the health care system."[2] Since 1997, CMS has contracted with Program Safeguard Contractors (PSCs) to detect and investigate potential Medicare fraud and abuse in Medicare Parts A and B. CMS is in the process of transitioning the PSC anti-fraud activities to newly established zone program integrity contractors (ZPICs), though the contract recipients are primarily the same entities with the same capabilities. Program integrity activities for all claim types (Medicare Parts A, B, C, and D) will now be conducted under a single ZPIC contract for each geographic area, or zone, of which there are seven across the country. CMS has informed this Committee that contracts have now been awarded to ZPICs for six of the seven zones. For Zone 6, the Northeast region, CMS asserted that the award is currently under protest and that "CMS is providing benefit integrity oversight and monitoring via the Program Safeguard Contractors."

Currently, the PSCs/ZPICs analyze data to identify improper billing patterns, perform provider audits, investigate fraud leads, refer cases to the HHS/Office of Inspector General (OIG) or U.S. Department of Justice (DOJ) for prosecution, and implement administrative actions to recover improper payments. PSCs/ZPICs do not collect overpayments, but refer suspected overpayments to claims processors, such as Medicare Administrative Contractors (MACs).

CMS also contracts with Medicare Drug Integrity Contractors (MEDICs) to conduct program integrity activities primarily in Medicare Part D. MEDICs perform similar functions as PSCs/ZPICs, including data analysis to identify patterns of erroneous billing, investigation, development of fraud and abuse cases, referral of cases to the HHS/OIG or DOJ for prosecution, and implementation of administrative actions.

In order to better understand the effectiveness of such efforts as well as determine whether CMS is conducting adequate oversight of these contractors, Subcommittee staff met on a bipartisan basis with officials from CMS. Documents provided by the agency revealed that from the beginning of 2009 through 2011, PSCs/ZPICs recovered only 10 percent of the overpayments they identified. These documents also showed that several performance measures used to track the contractors decreased from 2007 through 2011. The number of cases the contractors referred to law enforcement agencies, the total number of investigations initiated by the contractors, and the number of investigations the contractors developed through proactive data analysis all dropped substantially during this five-year period.

In addition, a study by HHS/OIG concluded that the overpayments PSCs identified and referred for collection did not result in significant recoveries to the Medicare program. The OIG found that the PSCs identified 4,239 overpayments totaling $835 million during 2007, but that only 7 percent of the overpayment amount had been collected by claims processors as of June 2008.[3] These figures highlight the challenges in recovering funds once fraud has occurred, and illustrate the need for contractors to engage in more proactive investigation to prevent fraud before the claims are paid.

III. Issues

The following issues will be examined at the hearing:

- CMS oversight of the PSCs/ZPICs, MACs and MEDICs;
- The performance of the program integrity contractors, including their effectiveness at identifying and recovering fraudulent overpayments, the number of proactive investigations they initiated, their use of provider suspension authorities, and their investigative referrals to law enforcement agencies; and,
- Ways to enhance the effectiveness of the program integrity contractors.

End Notes

[1] The Federal Bureau of Investigation (FBI) refers to estimates of 3-10% of all health care billings as potentially fraudulent, see Annual Financial Crimes Report available at http://www.fbi.gov/publications/financial report2008/financial crime 2008.htm#health.

[2] Department of Health and Human Services, Fiscal Year 2012 Centers for Medicare and Medicaid Services, Justification of Estimates for Appropriations Committees.

[3] HHS/OIG Report # 03-08-00030, "Collection Status of Medicare Overpayments Identified by Program Safeguard Contractors", pg.ii.

In: Fraud Detection and Deterrence ... ISBN: 978-1-62417-658-6
Editor: Anton Ferilli

Chapter 3

MEDICARE: PROGRESS MADE TO DETER FRAUD, BUT MORE COULD BE DONE. STATEMENT OF KATHLEEN M. KING, DIRECTOR, HEALTH CARE, GOVERNMENT ACCOUNTABILITY OFFICE. HEARING ON "MEDICARE CONTRACTORS' EFFORTS TO FIGHT FRAUD: MOVING BEYOND 'PAY AND CHASE'"*

United States Government Accountability Office

WHY GAO DID THIS STUDY

GAO has designated Medicare as a high-risk program. Since 1990, every two years GAO has provided Congress with an update on this program, which highlights government operations that are at high risk for waste, fraud, abuse mismanagement or in need of broad reform. Medicare has been included in this program in part because its complexity makes it particularly vulnerable to

* This is an edited, reformatted and augmented version of a Statement given on June 8, 2012 before the House Committee on Energy and Commerce, Subcommittee on Oversight and Investigations.

fraud. Fraud involves an intentional act or representation to deceive with the knowledge that the action or representation could result in gain. The deceptive nature of fraud makes its extent in the Medicare program difficult to measure in a reliable way, but it is clear that fraud contributes to Medicare's fiscal problems. Reducing fraud could help rein in the escalating costs of the program.

This statement focuses on the progress made and important steps to be taken by CMS and its program integrity contractors to reduce fraud in Medicare. These contractors perform functions such as screening and enrolling providers, detecting and investigating potential fraud, and identifying improper payments and vulnerabilities that could lead to payment errors. This statement is based on relevant GAO products and recommendations issued from 2004 through 2012 using a variety of methodologies, such as analyses of Medicare claims, review of relevant policies and procedures, and interviews with officials.

What GAO Found

The Centers for Medicare & Medicaid Services (CMS)—the agency that administers Medicare—has made progress in implementing several key strategies GAO identified in prior work as helpful in protecting Medicare from fraud; however, important actions that could help CMS and its program integrity contractors combat fraud remain incomplete.

Provider Enrollment: GAO's previous work found persistent weaknesses in Medicare's enrollment standards and procedures that increased the risk of enrolling entities intent on defrauding the program. CMS has strengthened provider enrollment—for example, in February 2011, CMS designated three levels of risk—high, moderate, and limited—with different screening procedures for categories of providers at each level. However, CMS has not completed other actions, including implementation of some relevant provisions of the Patient Protection and Affordable Care Act (PPACA). Specifically, CMS has not

1) determined which providers will be required to post surety bonds to help ensure that payments made for fraudulent billing can be recovered,
2) contracted for fingerprint-based criminal background checks,

3) issued a final regulation to require additional provider disclosures of information, and
4) established core elements for provider compliance programs.

Pre- and Post-payment Claims Review: GAO had previously found that increased efforts to review claims on a prepayment basis can prevent payments from being made for potentially fraudulent claims, while improving systems used by CMS and its contractors to review claims on a post-payment basis could better identify patterns of potentially fraudulent billing for further investigation. CMS has controls in Medicare's claims-processing systems to determine if claims should be paid, denied, or reviewed further. These controls require timely and accurate information about providers that GAO has previously recommended that CMS strengthen. GAO is currently examining CMS's new Fraud Prevention System, which uses analytic methods to examine claims before payment to develop investigative leads for Zone Program Integrity Contractors (ZPIC), the contractors responsible for detecting and investigating potential fraud. Additionally, CMS could improve its post-payment claims review to identify patterns of fraud by incorporating prior GAO recommendations to develop plans and timelines for fully implementing and expanding two information technology systems it developed.

Robust Process to Address Identified Vulnerabilities: Having mechanisms in place to resolve vulnerabilities that lead to erroneous payments is critical to effective program management and could help address fraud. Such vulnerabilities are service- or system-specific weaknesses that can lead to payment errors—for example, providers receiving multiple payments as a result of incorrect coding. GAO has previously identified weaknesses in CMS's process for addressing identified vulnerabilities and the Department of Health and Human Services' Office of Inspector General recently reported on CMS's inaction in addressing vulnerabilities identified by its contractors, including ZPICs. GAO is evaluating the current status of the process for assessing and developing corrective actions to address vulnerabilities.

Mr. Chairman, Ranking Member, and Other Members of the Committee:

I am pleased to be here today to discuss our work regarding fraud in the Medicare program, Medicare contractors' roles in detecting and preventing fraud, and provisions in recent laws and agency actions that may help address this problem.[1] Fraud involves an intentional act or representation to deceive with the knowledge that the action or representation could result in gain. Although there have been convictions for multi-million dollar schemes that defrauded the Medicare program, the extent of the problem is unknown. There are no reliable estimates of the extent of fraud in the Medicare program or for the health care industry as a whole. By its very nature, fraud is difficult to detect, as those involved are engaged in intentional deception. For example, fraud may involve providers submitting a claim with false documentation for services not provided, while the claim on its face may appear valid. Fraud also can involve efforts to hide ownership of companies or kickbacks to obtain beneficiary information. Although the full extent of the problem is unknown, it is clear that the Medicare program is vulnerable to fraud, which contributes to Medicare's fiscal problems. Reducing fraud could help rein in the escalating costs of the program.

We have repeatedly designated Medicare as a high-risk program, as its complexity and susceptibility to payment errors from various causes, added to its size, have made it vulnerable to loss. 2 As one example, the fee-for-service (FFS) portion of the Medicare program processes over a billion claims a year from about 1.5-million providers and suppliers; working to ensure that those payments are accurate is a complex, ongoing task. Medicare has many individual vulnerabilities, which are service- or system-specific weaknesses that can lead to payment errors, including those due to fraud.[3] If the Centers for Medicare & Medicaid Services (CMS), the agency within the Department of Health and Human Services (HHS) that administers the program, suspects that providers or suppliers are billing fraudulently, it can take action, including suspending claims payment, revoking billing privileges, or referring cases to law enforcement for investigation.[4] Further, it can impose a moratorium on new enrollment of providers or suppliers.[5] Since 1997, Congress has provided funds specifically for activities to address fraud, as well as waste and abuse,[6] in Medicare and other federal health care programs. In addition, Congress created the Medicare Integrity Program to conduct activities to reduce fraud, waste, abuse, and improper payments.[7] In 2010, Congress passed the Patient Protection and Affordable Care Act (PPACA), which provided additional funding for such efforts and set a number of new requirements specific to Medicare.[8] Furthermore, the Small Business Jobs Act of 2010[9] established new Medicare fee-forservice claims review requirements and provided funding to implement these requirements. My testimony today focuses on the progress made and steps that remain to be taken by CMS and its program integrity contractors to reduce fraud in Medicare. CMS contractors perform a number of key program integrity functions, such as screening and enrolling providers, detecting and investigating potential fraud, and identifying improper payments and vulnerabilities that could lead to payment errors. This testimony is informed by 8 years of our work on Medicare fraud, waste, abuse, and improper payments. I will focus on several key strategies CMS can undertake to help reduce fraud discussed in our prior work from 2004 to 2012, specifically:[10]

- strengthening provider enrollment standards and procedures,
- improving pre- and post-payment claims review, and
- developing a robust process for addressing identified vulnerabilities.

The products on which this statement is based were developed by using a variety of methodologies, including analyses of Medicare claims, review of relevant policies and procedures, interviews with agency officials and other stakeholders, and site visits.[11] The work on which these products were based was conducted in accordance with generally accepted government auditing standards. Those standards require that we plan and perform the audit to obtain sufficient, appropriate evidence to provide a reasonable basis for our findings and conclusions based on our audit objectives. We believe that the evidence obtained provides a reasonable basis for our findings and conclusions based on our audit objectives.

CMS Has Made Progress in Strengthening Provider Enrollment, but Further Actions Are Needed

CMS has made progress strengthening provider enrollment to try to better ensure that only legitimate providers and suppliers are allowed to bill Medicare. However, CMS has not completed other actions that could help prevent individuals intent on fraud from enrolling, including implementation of some relevant PPACA provisions.

Past CMS Efforts to Strengthen Provider Enrollment

Our previous work found persistent weaknesses in Medicare's enrollment standards and procedures that increased the risk of enrolling entities intent on defrauding the Medicare program.[12] We, CMS, and the HHS Office of Inspector General (OIG) have previously identified two types of providers whose services and items are especially vulnerable to improper payments and fraud—home health agencies (HHA) and suppliers of durable medical equipment, prosthetics, orthotics, and supplies (DMEPOS). We found weaknesses in oversight of these providers' and suppliers' enrollment. For example, in 2008, we identified weaknesses when we created two fictitious DMEPOS companies, which were subsequently enrolled by CMS's contractor and given permission to begin billing Medicare.[13] In 2009, we found that CMS's contractors were not requiring HHAs to resubmit enrollment information for re-verification every 5 years as required by CMS.[14]

To strengthen the Medicare enrollment process, in 2006 CMS began requiring all providers and suppliers—including those that order HHA services or DMEPOS for beneficiaries to be enrolled in Medicare. The agency also required all providers and suppliers to report their National Provider Identifiers (NPI) on enrollment applications, which can help address fraud because providers and suppliers must submit either their Social Security Number or their employer identification number and state licensing information to obtain an NPI.[15] In 2007, CMS initiated the first phase of a Medicare competitive-bidding program for DMEPOS.[16] This program requires suppliers' bids to include new financial documentation for the year prior to submitting the bids. Because CMS can now disqualify suppliers based in part on new scrutiny of their financial documents, competitive bidding can help reduce fraud. Finally, in 2010, CMS also required that all DMEPOS suppliers be accredited by a CMS-approved accrediting organization to ensure that they meet certain quality standards. Such accreditation also increased scrutiny of these businesses.

CMS Has Taken Action on Certain PPACA Provider Enrollment Provisions

PPACA authorized CMS to implement several actions to strengthen provider enrollment. As of April 2012, the agency has completed some of these actions.

Screening Provider Enrollment Applications by Risk Level

CMS and OIG issued a final rule with comment period in February 2011 to implement some of the new screening procedures required by PPACA.[17]

CMS designated three levels of risk—high, moderate, and limited—with different screening procedures for categories of Medicare providers at each level. Providers in the high-risk level are subject to the most rigorous screening.[18] To determine which providers to place in these risk levels, CMS considered issues such as past occurrences of improper payments and fraud among different categories of providers. Based in part on our work and that of the OIG, CMS designated newly enrolling HHAs and DMEPOS suppliers as high risk and designated other providers at lower levels. (See table 1.) Providers at all risk levels are screened to verify that they meet specific requirements established by Medicare such as having current licenses or accreditation and valid Social Security numbers.[19]

Table 1. Categories of Medicare Providers and Suppliers Designated by Risk Level for Enrollment Screening

Risk level	Categories of Medicare providers and suppliers
Limited	Physician or nonphysician practitioners and medical groups or clinics, with the exception of physical therapists and physical therapy groups. Ambulatory surgical centers, competitive acquisition programs/Part B vendors, end-stage renal disease facilities, federally qualified health centers, histocompatibility laboratories,[a] Indian Health Service facilities, mammography screening centers, mass immunization roster billers,[b] pharmacies newly enrolling or revalidating, radiation therapy centers, religious nonmedical health care institutions, rural health clinics, skilled nursing facilities, and hospitals, including critical access hospitals.
Moderate	Ambulance suppliers, community mental health centers, comprehensive outpatient rehabilitation facilities, hospice organizations, independent diagnostic testing facilities, independent clinical laboratories, portable X-ray suppliers, currently enrolled (revalidating) home health agencies, and physical therapy, including physical therapy groups.
High	Prospective (newly enrolling) home health agencies and prospective (newly enrolling) suppliers of durable medical equipment, prosthetics, orthotics, and supplies.

Source: GAO analysis of CMS Final Rule with Comment Period, Medicare, Medicaid, and Children's Health Insurance Programs: Additional Screening Requirements, Applications Fees, Temporary Enrollment Moratoria, Payment Suspensions and Compliance Plans for Providers and Suppliers, 76 Fed. Reg. 5862 (Feb. 2, 2011).

[a]Histocompatibility laboratories provide evaluations of certain genetic data and pertinent patient immunologic risk factors to allow clinician and patient to make decisions about whether transplantation is in the patient's best interest.

[b]Mass immunization roster billers are providers and suppliers that enroll in the Medicare program to offer influenza (flu) vaccinations to a large number of individuals, and these entities must be properly licensed in the states in which they plan to operate influenza clinics.

High- and moderate-risk providers are additionally subject to unannounced site visits. Further, depending on the risks presented, PPACA authorizes CMS to require fingerprint-based criminal history checks, and the posting of surety bonds for certain providers.[20] CMS may also provide enhanced oversight for specific periods for new providers and for initial claims of DMEPOS suppliers.

CMS indicated that the agency will continue to review the criteria for its screening levels on an ongoing basis and would publish changes if the agency decided to update the assignment of screening levels for categories of Medicare providers. This may become necessary because fraud is not confined to HHAs and DMEPOS suppliers.

We are currently examining the types of providers involved in fraud cases investigated by the OIG and the Department of Justice (DOJ), which may help illuminate risk to the Medicare program from different types of providers.

Further, in their 2011 annual report on the Health Care Fraud and Abuse Control Program, DOJ and HHS reported convictions or other legal actions, such as exclusions or civil monetary penalties, against several types of Medicare providers other than DMEPOS suppliers and HHAs, including pharmacists, orthopedic surgeons, infusion and other types of medical clinics, and physical therapy services.[21] CMS also has established triggers for adjustments to an individual provider's risk level. For example, CMS regulations state that an individual provider or supplier at the limited- or moderate-risk level that has had its billing privileges revoked by a Medicare contractor within the last 10 years and is attempting to re-enroll, would move to the high-risk level for screening.

New National Enrollment Screening and Site Visit Contractors

In a further effort to strengthen its enrollment processes, CMS contracted with two new entities at the end of 2011 to assume centralized responsibility for automated screening of provider and supplier enrollment and for conducting site visits of providers.

- **Automated-screening contractor**. In December 2011, the new contractor began to establish systems to conduct automated screening of providers and suppliers to ensure they meet Medicare eligibility criteria (such as valid licensure, accreditation, a valid NPI, and no presence on the OIG list of providers and suppliers excluded from participating in federal health care programs).[22] Prior to the implementation of this new automated screening, such screening was done manually for the 30,000 enrollees each month by CMS's Medicare Administrative Contractors (MAC), which enroll Medicare providers, and the National Supplier Clearinghouse (NSC), which enrolls DMEPOS suppliers. According to CMS, the old screening process was neither efficient nor timely. CMS officials said that in 2012, the automated-screening contractor began automated screening of the licensure status of all currently enrolled Medicare providers and suppliers.

The agency said it expects the automated-screening contractor to begin screening newly enrolling providers and suppliers later this year. CMS expects that the new, national contractor will enable better monitoring of providers and suppliers on a continuous basis to help ensure they continue to meet Medicare enrollment requirements. The new screening contractor will also help the MACs and the NSC maintain enrollment information in CMS's Provider Enrollment Chain and Ownership System (PECOS)—a database that contains details on enrolled providers and suppliers. In addition, CMS officials said the automated-screening contractor is developing an individual risk score for each provider or supplier, similar to a credit risk score. Although these individual scores are not currently used to determine an individual provider's placement in a risk level, CMS indicated that this risk score may be used eventually as additional risk criteria in the screening process.

- **Site visits for all providers designated as moderate and high risk.** Beginning in February 2012, a single national site-visit contractor began conducting site visits of moderate- and high-risk providers to determine if sites are legitimate and the providers meet certain Medicare standards.[23]

  The contractor collects the same information from each site visit, including photographic evidence that will be available electronically through a Web portal accessible to CMS and its other contractors. The national site-visit contractor is expected to validate the legitimacy of these sites. CMS officials told us that the contractor will provide consistency in site visits across the country, in contrast to CMS relying on different MACs to conduct any required site visits.

CMS Has Not Completely Implemented Some PPACA Enrollment Provisions

Implementation of other enrollment screening actions authorized by PPACA that could help CMS reduce the enrollment of providers and suppliers intent on defrauding the Medicare program remains incomplete, including:

- ***Surety bond***—PPACA authorizes CMS to require a surety bond for certain types of at-risk providers, which can be helpful in recouping erroneous payments. CMS officials expect to issue a proposed rule to require surety bonds as conditions of enrollment for certain other types of providers. Extending the use of surety bonds to these new entities would augment a previous statutory requirement for DMEPOS suppliers to post a surety bond at the time of enrollment.[24] CMS issued final instructions to its MACs, effective February 2012, for recovering DMEPOS overpayments through surety bonds. CMS officials reported that as of April 19, 2012, they had issued notices to 20 surety bond companies indicating intent to collect funds, but had not collected any funds as of that date.
- ***Fingerprint-based criminal background checks***—CMS officials told us that they are working with the Federal Bureau of Investigation to arrange contracts to help conduct fingerprint-based criminal background checks of high-risk providers and suppliers. On April 13, 2012, CMS issued a request for information regarding the potential solicitation of a single contract for Medicare provider and supplier fingerprint-based background checks. The agency expects to have the contract in place before the end of 2012.
- ***Providers and suppliers disclosure***—CMS officials said the agency is reviewing options to include in regulations for increased disclosures of prior actions taken against providers and suppliers enrolling or revalidating enrollment in Medicare, such as whether the provider or supplier has been subject to a payment suspension from a federal health care program.[25] In April 2012, agency officials indicated that they were not certain when the regulation would be published. CMS officials noted that the additional disclosure requirements are complicated by provider and supplier concerns about what types of information will be collected, what CMS will do with it, and how the privacy and security of this information will be maintained.

- ***Compliance and ethics program***—CMS officials said that the agency was studying criteria found in OIG model plans as it worked to address the PPACA requirement that the agency establish the core elements of compliance programs for providers and suppliers.[26] As of April 2012, CMS did not have a projected target date for implementation.

Additional Action May Help Better Identify Potential Fraud through Pre- and Post- Payment Claims Review

Increased efforts to review claims on a prepayment basis can better prevent payments that should not be made, while improving systems used to review claims on a post-payment basis could better identify patterns of fraudulent billing for further investigation.

Additional Efforts to Improve Prepayment Claims Review May Help Reduce Fraud

Having robust controls in claims payment systems to prevent payment of problematic claims can help reduce loss. As claims go through Medicare's electronic claims payment systems, they are subjected to automated prepayment controls called "edits," instructions programmed in the systems to prevent payment of incomplete or incorrect claims. Some edits use provider enrollment information, while others use information on coverage or payment policies, to determine if claims should be paid. Most of these controls are fully automated; if a claim does not meet the criteria of the edit, it is automatically denied. Other prepayment edits are manual; they flag a claim for individual review by trained staff who determine if it should be paid. Due to the volume of claims, CMS has reported that less than 1 percent of Medicare claims are subject to manual medical record review by trained staff.

Having effective pre-payment edits that deny claims for ineligible providers and suppliers depends on having timely and accurate information about them, such as whether the providers are currently enrolled and have the appropriate license or accreditation to provide specific services. We previously recommended that CMS take action to ensure the timeliness and accuracy of

PECOS—the database that maintains Medicare provider and supplier enrollment information. We noted that weaknesses in PECOS data may result in CMS making improper payments to ineligible providers and suppliers.[27] These weaknesses are related to the frequency with which CMS's contractors update enrollment information and the timeliness and accuracy of information obtained from outside entities, such as state licensing boards, the OIG, and the Social Security Administration's Death Master File, which contains information on deceased individuals that can be used to identify deceased providers in order to terminate those providers' Medicare billing privileges. These sources vary in the ease in which CMS contractors have been able to access their data and the frequency with which they are updated. CMS has indicated that its new national-screening contractor should improve the timeliness and accuracy of the provider and supplier information in PECOS by centralizing the process, increasing automation of the process, continuously checking databases, and incorporating new sources of data, such as financial, business, tax, and geospatial data. However, it is too soon to tell if these efforts will better prevent payments to ineligible providers and suppliers.

Having effective edits to implement coverage and payment policies before payment is made can also help to deter fraud. The Medicare program has defined categories of items and services eligible for coverage and excludes from coverage items or services that are determined not to be "reasonable and necessary for the diagnosis and treatment of an illness or injury or to improve functioning of a malformed body part." [28] CMS and its contractors set policies regarding when and how items and services will be covered by Medicare, as well as coding and billing requirements for payment, which also can be implemented in the payment systems through edits. We have previously found Medicare's payment systems did not have edits for items and services unlikely to be provided in the normal course of medical care.[29] CMS has since implemented edits to flag such claims—called Medically Unlikely Edits. We are currently assessing Medicare's prepayment edits based on coverage and payment policies, including the Medically Unlikely Edits.

Additionally, suspending payments to providers suspected of fraudulent billing can be an effective tool to prevent excess loss to the Medicare program while suspected fraud is being investigated. For example, in March 2011, the OIG testified that payment suspensions and prepayment edits on 18 providers and suppliers stopped the potential loss of more than $1.3 million submitted in claims by these individuals. Furthermore, HHS recently reported that it imposed payment suspensions on 78 home health agencies in conjunction with arrests related to a multimillion-dollar health care fraud scheme. While CMS had the authority to impose payment suspensions prior to PPACA, the law specifically authorized CMS to suspend payments to providers pending the investigation of credible allegations of fraud.[30] CMS officials reported that the agency had imposed 212 payment suspensions since the regulations implementing the PPACA provisions took effect. Agency officials indicated that almost half of these suspensions were imposed this calendar year, representing about $6 million in Medicare claims.

We are currently evaluating a new CMS effort, the Fraud Prevention System (FPS), which uses predictive analytic technologies to analyze FFS claims on a prepayment basis to develop investigative leads for CMS's Zone Program Integrity Contractors (ZPIC), the contractors responsible for detecting and investigating potential fraud.[31] The Small Business Jobs Act of 2010 requires CMS to use predictive analytic technologies both to identify and to prevent improper payments under Medicare FFS.[32] The law requires these predictive analytic technologies to be used to review claims for potential fraud by identifying unusual or suspicious patterns or abnormalities in Medicare provider networks, claims billing patterns, and beneficiary utilization. According to CMS, FPS may enhance CMS's ability to identify potential fraud because it analyzes large numbers of claims from multiple data sources nationwide simultaneously before payment is made, thus allowing CMS to examine billing patterns across geographic regions for those that may indicate fraud. The results of FPS are used by the ZPICs to initiate investigations that could result in payment suspensions, implementation of automatic claim denials, identification of additional prepayment edits, or the revocation of Medicare billing privileges. CMS began using FPS to screen all FFS claims nationwide prior to payment as of June 30, 2011, and CMS has been directing the ZPICs to investigate high priority leads generated by the system. Because FPS is relatively new and we have not completed our work, it is too soon to determine whether FPS will improve CMS's ability to address fraud. Questions have also been raised about CMS's ability to adequately assess ZPICs' performance and we have been asked to examine CMS's management of the ZPICs, including criteria used by CMS to evaluate their effectiveness.

"Bust-out" fraud schemes in which providers or suppliers suddenly bill very high volumes of claims to obtain large payments from Medicare could be addressed by adding a prepayment edit. Such an edit would set thresholds to stop payment for atypically rapid increases in billing thus helping them to stem losses from these schemes. In our prior work on DMEPOS, we recommended that CMS require its contractors to develop thresholds for unexplained increases in billing and use them to develop pre-payment controls that could suspend these claims for further review before payment.[33] CMS officials told us that they are currently considering developing analytic models in FPS that could help CMS and ZPICs identify and address billing practices suggestive of bust outs.

Actions Needed to Improve Use of Systems Intended for Post-payment Claims Review

Further actions are needed to improve use of two CMS information technology systems that could help CMS and program integrity contractors identify fraud after claims have been paid.[34]

- The Integrated Data Repository (IDR) became operational in September 2006 as a central data store of Medicare and other data needed to help CMS's program integrity staff, ZPICs, and other contractors prevent and detect improper payments of claims. However, we found IDR did not include all the data that were planned to be incorporated by fiscal year 2010, because of technical obstacles and delays in funding. Further, as of December 2011 the agency had not finalized plans or developed reliable schedules for efforts to incorporate these data, which could lead to additional delays.
- One Program Integrity (One PI) is a Web portal intended to provide CMS staff, ZPICs, and other contractors with a single source of access to data contained in IDR, as well as tools for analyzing those data. While One PI is operational, we reported in December 2011 that CMS had trained few program integrity analysts and that the system was not being widely used.

GAO recommended that CMS take steps to finalize plans and reliable schedules for fully implementing and expanding the use of both IDR and One PI. Although the agency told us in April 2012 that it had initiated activities to incorporate some additional data into IDR and expand the use of One PI, such as training more ZPIC and other staff, it has not fully addressed our recommendations.

A Robust Process to Address Identified Vulnerabilities Could Help Reduce Fraud

Having mechanisms in place to resolve vulnerabilities that lead to improper payments is critical to effective program management and could help address fraud.[35] A number of different types of program integrity contractors are responsible for identifying and reporting vulnerabilities to CMS. However, our work and the work of OIG have shown weaknesses in CMS's processes to address vulnerabilities identified by these contractors.

CMS's Recovery Audit Contractors (RAC) are specifically charged with identifying improper payments and vulnerabilities that could lead to such payment errors. However, in our March 2010 report on the RAC demonstration program, we found that CMS had not established an adequate process during the demonstration or in planning for the national program to ensure prompt resolution of such identified vulnerabilities in Medicare; further, the majority of the most significant vulnerabilities identified during the demonstration were not addressed.[36] We therefore recommended that CMS develop and implement a corrective action process that includes policies and procedures to ensure the agency promptly (1) evaluates findings of RAC audits, (2) decides on the appropriate response and a time frame for taking action based on established criteria, and (3) acts to correct the vulnerabilities identified.[37]

Our recommendations will not be fully addressed until CMS has put policies and procedures in place that will lead the agency to act promptly to correct identified vulnerabilities. In December 2011, the OIG similarly found that CMS lacked procedures to ensure that vulnerabilities identified by other contractors were resolved.[38] CMS had not resolved or taken significant action to resolve 38 of 44 vulnerabilities (86 percent) reported in 2009 by ZPICs. Only 1 vulnerability had been fully resolved by January 2011.[39] The OIG made several recommendations, including that CMS have written procedures and time frames to assure that vulnerabilities were resolved. CMS has indicated that it is now tracking vulnerabilities identified from several types of contractors through a single vulnerability tracking process. We are currently examining aspects of CMS's vulnerability tracking process and will be reporting on it soon.

CONCLUSION

Although CMS has taken some important steps to identify and prevent fraud, including implementing provisions in PPACA and the Small Business Jobs Act, more remains to be done to prevent making erroneous Medicare payments due to fraud. In particular, we have found CMS could do more to strengthen provider enrollment screening to avoid enrolling those intent on committing fraud, improve pre- and post-payment claims review to identify and respond to patterns of suspicious billing activity more effectively, and identify and address vulnerabilities to reduce the ease with which fraudulent entities can obtain improper payments. It is critical that CMS implement and make full use of new authorities granted by recent legislation, as well as incorporate recommendations made by us, as well as the OIG in these areas. Moving from responding once fraud has already occurred to preventing it from occurring in the first place is key to ensuring that federal funds are used efficiently and for their intended purposes.

As all of these new authorities and requirements become part of Medicare's operations, additional evaluation and oversight will be necessary to determine whether they are implemented as required and have the desired effect. We have several studies underway that assess efforts to fight fraud in Medicare and that should continue to help CMS refine and improve its fraud detection and prevention efforts. Notably, we are assessing the effectiveness of different types of pre-payment edits in Medicare and of CMS's oversight of its contractors in implementing those edits to help ensure that Medicare pays claims correctly the first time. We are also examining the use of predictive analytics by CMS and the ZPICs to improve fraud prevention and detection. ZPICs play an important role in detecting and investigating fraud and identifying vulnerabilities, and FPS will likely play an increasing role in how ZPICs conduct their work. Additionally, we have work under way to identify the types of providers and suppliers currently under investigation and those that have been found to have engaged in fraudulent activities. These studies may enable us to point out additional actions for CMS that could help the agency more systematically reduce fraud in the Medicare program.

Due to the amount of program funding at risk, fraud will remain a continuing threat to Medicare, so continuing vigilance to reduce vulnerabilities will be necessary. Individuals who want to defraud Medicare will continue to develop new approaches to try to circumvent CMS's safeguards and investigative and enforcement efforts. Although targeting certain types of providers that the agency has identified as high risk may be useful, it may allow other types of providers committing fraud to go unnoticed. We will continue to assess efforts to fight fraud and provide recommendations to CMS, as appropriate, that we believe will assist the agency and its contractors in this important task. We urge CMS to continue its efforts as well.

Mr. Chairman, this concludes my prepared statement. I would be happy to answer any questions you or other members of the committee may have.

End Notes

[1] Medicare is the federally financed health insurance program for persons age 65 or over, certain individuals with disabilities, and individuals with end-stage renal disease. Medicare Parts A and B are known as Medicare fee-for-service (FFS). Medicare Part A covers hospital and other inpatient stays. Medicare Part B is optional, and covers hospital outpatient, physician, and other services. Medicare beneficiaries have the option of obtaining coverage for Medicare services from private health plans that participate in Medicare Advantage—Medicare's managed care program—also known as Part C. All Medicare beneficiaries may purchase coverage for outpatient prescription drugs under Part D, either as a stand-alone benefit or as part of a Medicare Advantage plan.

[2] In 1990, we began to report on government operations that we identified as "high risk" for serious weaknesses in areas that involve substantial resources and provide critical services to the public. Medicare has been included among such programs since 1990. See GAO, *High-Risk Series: An Update*, GAO-11-278 (Washington, D.C.: February 2011). http://www.gao.gov/highrisk/risks

[3] CMS defines vulnerabilities to the Medicare program as issues that can lead to fraud, waste, or abuse, which can either be specific, such as providers receiving multiple payments as a result of incorrect coding for a service, or general and programwide, such as weaknesses in online application processes.

[4] In this testimony, the term *provider* includes entities such as hospitals or physicians, and *supplier* means an entity that supplies Medicare beneficiaries with durable medical equipment, prosthetics, orthotics, and supplies (DMEPOS) such as walkers and wheelchairs.

[5] Enrolling as a provider or supplier in Medicare allows an entity to provide services or equipment to beneficiaries and bill for those services.

[6] Waste includes inaccurate payments for services, such as unintentional duplicate payments. Abuse represents actions inconsistent with acceptable business or medical practices.

[7] An improper payment is any payment that should not have been made or that was made in an incorrect amount (including overpayments and underpayments) under statutory, contractual, administrative, or other legally applicable requirements. This definition includes any payment to an ineligible recipient, any payment for an ineligible good or service, any duplicate payment, any payment for a good or service not received (except where authorized by law), and any payment that does not account for credit for applicable discounts. Improper Payments Elimination and Recovery Act of 2010, Pub. L. No. 111-204, § 2(e), 124 Stat. 2224, 2227 (codified at 31 U.S.C. § 3321 note).

[8] Pub. L. No. 111-148, 124 Stat.119 (2010), as amended by Health Care and Education Reconciliation Act of 2010 (HCERA), Pub. L. No. 111-152, 124 Stat. 1029, which we refer to collectively as PPACA. The provisions discussed in this statement are generally located

in sections 6401 through 6411 and 10603 and 10605 of PPACA, as well as sections 1303 and 1304 of HCERA.

[9] Pub. L. No. 111-240, § 4241, 124 Stat. 2504, 2599.

[10] These strategies were among those identified in our June 2010 testimony as critical to helping prevent fraud, waste, and abuse in Medicare. See GAO, *Medicare Fraud, Waste, and Abuse: Challenges and Strategies for Preventing Improper Payments,* GAO-10-844T (Washington, D.C.: June 15, 2010). A list of related products appears at the end of this statement.

[11] The products listed at the end of this statement contain detailed information on the methodologies used in our work.

[12] See GAO, *Medicare: CMS's Program Safeguards Did Not Deter Growth in Spending for Power Wheelchairs*; GAO-05-43 (Washington, D.C.: Nov. 17, 2004); *Medicare: More Effective Screening and Stronger Enrollment Standards Needed for Medical Equipment Suppliers*, GAO-05-656 (Washington, D.C.: Sept. 22, 2005); *Medicare: Improvements Needed to Address Improper Payments for Medical Equipment and Supplies*, GAO-07-59 (Washington, D.C.: Jan. 31, 2007); and *Medicare: Improvements Needed to Address Improper Payments in Home Health*, GAO-09-185 (Washington, D.C.: Feb. 27, 2009).

[13] GAO, *Medicare: Covert Testing Exposes Weaknesses in the Durable Medical Equipment Supplier Screening Process*, GAO-08-955 (Washington, D.C.: July 3, 2008).

[14] GAO-09-185.

[15] The Health Insurance Portability and Accountability Act of 1996 required that HHS adopt standards for unique health identifiers. CMS adopted the NPI as the standard unique health identifier for its health care providers and suppliers in its final rule: HIPAA Administrative Simplification: Standard Unique Health Identifier for Health Care Providers, 69 Fed. Reg. 3434 (Jan. 23, 2004). Consistent with the NPI final rule, beginning in 2006, the Medicare program required providers and suppliers to report their NPIs on their enrollment applications.

[16] Competitive bidding is a process in which suppliers of medical equipment and supplies compete for the right to provide their products on the basis of established criteria, such as quality and price.

[17] Medicare, Medicaid, and Children's Health Insurance Programs; Additional Screening Requirements, Application Fees, Temporary Enrollment Moratoria, Payment Suspensions and Compliance Plans for Providers and Suppliers, 76 Fed. Reg. 5862 (Feb. 2, 2011). In discussing the final rule, CMS noted that Medicare had already employed a number of the screening practices described in PPACA to determine if a provider is in compliance with federal and state requirements to enroll or to maintain enrollment in the Medicare program.

[18] PPACA specified that the enhanced-screening procedures would apply to new providers and suppliers beginning 1 year after the date of enactment and to currently enrolled providers and suppliers 2 years after that date.

[19] Screening may include verification of the following: Social Security number; NPI; National Practitioner Databank licensure; whether the provider has been excluded from federal health care programs by the OIG; taxpayer identification number; and death of an individual practitioner, owner, authorized official, delegated official, or supervising physician.

[20] A surety bond is a three-party agreement in which a company, known as a surety, agrees to compensate the bondholder if the bond purchaser fails to keep a specified promise.

[21] *The Department of Health and Human Services and the Department of Justice Health Care Fraud and Abuse Control Program Annual Report for Fiscal Year 2011* (Washington, D.C.: February 2012).

[22] Licensure is a mandatory process by which a state government grants permission to an individual practitioner or health care organization to engage in an occupation or profession.

[23] Starting March 25, 2011, CMS required the MACs to conduct site visits for categories of providers and suppliers designated as moderate and high risk. The national site-visit contactor assumed these responsibilities in 2012. The NSC will continue to conduct site visits related to provider enrollment of DMEPOS suppliers. In addition, CMS at times exercises its authority to conduct a site visit or requests its contractors to conduct a site visit for any Medicare provider or supplier.

[24] 42 U.S.C. § 1395m(a)(16)(B). As of October 2009, DMEPOS suppliers were required to obtain and submit a surety bond in the amount of at least $50,000. A DMEPOS surety bond is a bond issued by an entity guaranteeing that a DMEPOS supplier will fulfill its obligation to Medicare. If the obligation is not met, the surety bond is paid to Medicare. *Medicare Program; Surety Bond Requirement for Suppliers of Durable Medical Equipment, Prosthetics, Orthotics, and Supplies (DMEPOS)*, 74 *Fed. Reg.* 166 (Jan. 2, 2009).

[25] At the time of initial enrollment or revalidation of enrollment, PPACA requires providers and suppliers to disclose any current or previous affiliation with another provider or supplier that has uncollected debt; has been or is subject to a payment suspension under a federal health care program; has been excluded from participation under Medicare, Medicaid, or the State Children's Health Insurance Program; or has had its billing privileges denied or revoked. Pub. L. No. 111-148, § 6401(a)(4), 124 Stat. 119, 740 (2010).

[26] A compliance program is an internal set of policies, processes, and procedures that a provider organization implements to help it act ethically and lawfully. In this context, a compliance program is intended to help provider and supplier organizations prevent and detect violations of Medicare laws and regulations. CMS has used the phrase "compliance and ethics program" and indicated it may base its program on the seven elements of effective compliance and ethics programs found in the U.S. Federal Sentencing Guidelines Manual.

[27] GAO-12-351.

[28] 42 U.S.C. § 1395y(a)(1)(A).

[29] GAO-07-59.

[30] CMS is required to consult with the HHS OIG in determining whether a credible allegation of fraud exists. Based on how CMS used its previous payment suspension authority, in November 2010, the OIG found weaknesses in CMS's implementation of payment suspensions that could lead to delays in the suspension process. Such delays would allow payments to continue to providers suspected of fraud. Specifically, the OIG found that CMS's guidance to its contractors on procedures for implementing payment suspensions was incomplete and inconsistent. Although the OIG made no recommendations, it suggested that these weaknesses could be addressed through CMS rulemaking pursuant to PPACA.

[31] CMS is replacing its legacy Program Safeguard Contractors (PSC) with seven ZPICs. While the PSCs were responsible for program integrity for specific parts of Medicare, such as Part A, the ZPICs are responsible for Medicare's fee-for-service program integrity in their geographic zones. For simplicity, we refer to these program integrity contractors as ZPICs throughout the testimony.

[32] Pub. L. No. 111-240, § 4241, 124 Stat. 2504, 2599.

[33] See GAO, *2012 Annual Report: Opportunities to Reduce Duplication, Overlap and Fragmentation, Achieve Savings, and Enhance Revenue.* GAO-12-342SP (Washington, D.C.: Feb. 28, 2012) and GAO-07-59.

[34] GAO, *Fraud Detection Systems: Centers for Medicare and Medicaid Services Needs to Ensure More Widespread Use,* GAO-11-475 (Washington, D.C.: June 30, 2011).

[35] We have reported that an agency should have policies and procedures to ensure that (1) the findings of all audits and reviews are promptly evaluated, (2) decisions are made about the appropriate response to these findings, and (3) actions are taken to correct or resolve the issues promptly. These are all aspects of internal control, which is the component of an organization's management that provides reasonable assurance that the organization achieves effective and efficient operations, reliable financial reporting, and compliance with applicable laws and regulations. Internal control standards provide a framework for identifying and addressing major performance challenges and areas at greatest risk for mismanagement. GAO, *Internal Control Standards: Internal Control Management and Evaluation Tool,* GAO-01-1008G (Washington, D.C.: August 2001).

[36] GAO, *Medicare Recovery Audit Contracting: Weaknesses Remain in Addressing Vulnerabilities to Improper Payments, Although Improvements Made to Contractor Oversight,* GAO-10-143 (Washington, D.C.: Mar. 31, 2010).

[37] GAO-10-143.

[38] HHS-OIG, *Addressing Vulnerabilities Reported by Medicare Benefit Integrity Contractors,* OEI-03-10-00500 (December 2011).

[39] OIG also found that CMS had not resolved or taken significant action to resolve 10 of 18 vulnerabilities (56 percent) reported in 2009 by Medicare Prescription Drug Integrity Contractors (MEDICs)—program integrity contractors for Medicare Parts C and D. Only 1 of those 18 vulnerabilities had been fully resolved by January 2011.

In: Fraud Detection and Deterrence ...
Editor: Anton Ferilli
ISBN: 978-1-62417-658-6

Chapter 4

STATEMENT OF TED DOOLITTLE, DEPUTY DIRECTOR, CENTER FOR PROGRAM INTEGRITY, DEPARTMENT OF HEALTH AND HUMAN SERVICES. HEARING ON "MEDICARE CONTRACTORS' EFFORTS TO FIGHT FRAUD: MOVING BEYOND 'PAY AND CHASE'"*

Chairman Stearns, Ranking Member DeGette, and Members of the Subcommittee, thank you for the invitation to discuss the Centers for Medicare & Medicaid Services' (CMS) program integrity efforts and its management of its contractors for the Medicare program. The Administration has made important strides in reducing fraud, waste, and improper payments across the government. Over the last two years, CMS has implemented powerful new anti-fraud tools provided by Congress, as well as designed and implemented large-scale, innovative improvements to our Medicare program integrity strategy to shift beyond a "pay and chase" approach to preventing fraud. CMS' antifraud contractors are integral to our efforts to fight fraud and reduce improper payments.

---

* This is an edited, reformatted and augmented version of a Statement given on June 8, 2012 before the House Committee on Energy and Commerce, Subcommittee on Oversight and Investigations.

CMS Fee-for-Service Antifraud Contractors

CMS' mission is to ensure health care security for all Medicare, Medicaid, and Children's Health Insurance Program (CHIP) beneficiaries. A major component in achieving this mission is the successful administration of Original Medicare, commonly known as fee-for-service (FFS) Medicare. The Medicare FFS program represents the majority of Medicare spending, with hospital and other institutional services representing the largest spending outlays.

CMS uses a variety of different contractors to administer and oversee the Medicare fee-forservice program. Each of these contractors has different roles and responsibilities. Some contractors specifically assist CMS in combating fraud and identifying improper payments, while others assist CMS' fraud fighting efforts as part of their broader responsibilities as fee-forservice contractors who process claims and recover overpayments. The antifraud contractors do not perform any inherently governmental functions. Their actions are performed consistent with detailed standards and guidance provided by the agency to perform an administrative function in support of the agency's mission.

The CMS' Office of Acquisition and Grants Management (OAGM) procures these contracts and the contracts are subject to Federal contracting laws and regulations. Once any procurement is finalized, contractor management is handled by the CMS component with primary responsibility based on the contractor's core functions. CMS' program integrity strategy is moving away from pay and chase toward a more effective strategy that identifies fraud before payments are made, keeps bad providers and suppliers out of Medicare in the first place, quickly removes wrongdoers from the program once they are detected, and recovers improper payments as early and swiftly as possible. This approach builds upon CMS' use of Medicare Administrative Contractors, Zone Program Integrity Contractors, and Recovery Audit Contractors. A description of each of these contractors is below:

Medicare Administrative Contractors (MACs)

MACs are the central point of contact for providers within the national fee-for-service program. CMS' Center for Medicare directly oversees MACs. MACs are the entities responsible for provider and supplier screening and enrollment, and they process approximately 19,000 provider and supplier enrollment applications per month to determine whether these entities meet the requirements to receive billing privileges. MACs also audit the hospital cost reports upon which CMS bases Medicare reimbursements to hospitals. CMS directs the MACs to revoke provider and supplier billing privileges when CMS, the ZPICs, or MAC data shows it as appropriate. In CY 2011, as CMS took steps to reduce vulnerabilities in the Medicare program, CMS revoked the billing privileges of 4,850 providers and suppliers, and deactivated 56,733 billing numbers.

The MACs process, approve, and deny enrollment applications according to the enrollment standards established by CMS. MACs process 4.5 million claims each day, totaling approximately 1.2 billion claims in fiscal year (FY) 2011, and handle the first level of a provider's claim appeal. They implement all Medicare payment system changes, and conduct regular training and outreach to providers to educate them on proper claims coding and new Medicare payment policies. While MACs focus on claims processing and enrollment activities generally, they also play important roles in CMS' anti-fraud efforts. For instance, MACs put automated edits in place to identify and address claim coding errors, mutually exclusive claims, or medically unlikely claims. MACs regularly analyze claims data received to identify providers and suppliers with patterns of errors or unusually high volumes of particular claims types, and to develop additional prepayment edits. MACs coordinate the timing and implementation of these edits with other contractors. When MACs do identity potential fraud, they send the leads to the antifraud contractors to investigate further.

Zone Program Integrity Contractors (ZPICs)

CMS has nearly completed the process of transitioning from Program Safeguard Contractors (PSCs) to Zone Program Integrity Contractors (ZPICs). CMS created seven program integrity zones to align with the MAC jurisdictions. The ZPICs focus exclusively on a wide range of program integrity issues and projects. Six of the seven ZPICs have been awarded. The ZPICs and remaining PSC perform program integrity functions in these zones. The Center for Program Integrity within CMS directly manages the ZPICs. The ZPICs' main responsibilities are to:

- Develop investigative leads generated by the new Fraud Prevention System (FPS) and a variety of other sources;
- Perform data analysis to identify cases of suspected fraud, waste, and abuse;
- Make recommendations to CMS for appropriate administrative actions to protect Medicare Trust Fund dollars;
- Make referrals to law enforcement for potential prosecution;
- Provide support for ongoing investigations;
- Provide feedback and support to CMS to improve the FPS; and
- Identify improper payments to be recovered.

Unlike the MACs, the ZPICs' activities are dedicated exclusively to the prevention, detection, and recovery of potential fraud, waste, or abuse. The ZPICs coordinate with the MACs to implement administrative actions, including claim edits, payment suspensions, and revocations. ZPICs also refer overpayments to the MACs for collection. During 2011, CMS saved $208 million by denying claims through pre-payment edits that ZPICs recommended to automatically stop improper claims before they are paid. ZPIC-recommended payment suspensions led to over $27 million in recoveries against providers with overpayment demands.

Recovery Audit Contractors (RACs)

RACs' primary responsibilities are to identify a wide range of improper payments – including, but not limited to fraud – and to make recommendations to CMS about how to reduce improper payments in the Medicare program. In the fee-for-service Medicare program, RACs have identified several vulnerabilities where CMS has implemented corrective actions to prevent future improper payments. For example, CMS' contractors have implemented edits to stop the payment of claims provided after a beneficiary's date of death, stop the payment of durable medical equipment claims while the beneficiary is receiving care in an inpatient setting, and stop the payment for individual services that should have been bundled into another payment. If RACs identify or uncover potential fraud, they are required to report it directly to CMS, and to refrain from reviewing claims that are subject to an ongoing fraud investigation. In FY 2011, Medicare fee-for-service RACs collected nearly $797 million in overpayments, and already in the first half of FY 2012, Medicare fee-for-service RACs collected nearly $1 billion in overpayments.

Figure 1 below shows how CMS and its contractors communicate with each other during three key points within the Medicare fee-for-service process.

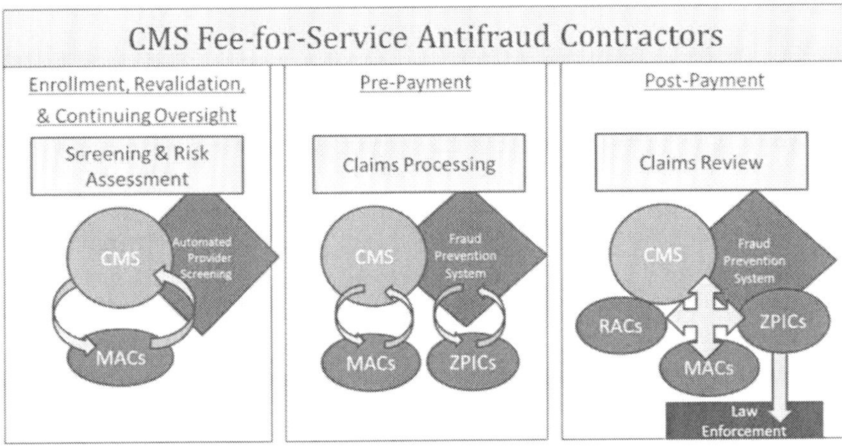

Figure 1.

Moving Beyond Pay and Chase: The Twin Pillar Strategy

CMS has recently implemented a twin pillar approach for advancing our fraud prevention strategy in Medicare. The first pillar is the new Fraud Prevention System (FPS) that applies predictive analytic technology on claims prior to payment to identify aberrant and suspicious billing patterns. The second pillar is the Automated Provider Screening (APS) system that is identifying ineligible providers and suppliers prior to enrollment or revalidation. Together, these two innovative, comprehensive new systems (the FPS and APS) are growing in their capacity to protect patients and taxpayers from those intent on defrauding our programs. These pillars represent an integrated approach to program integrity – preventing fraud before payments are made, keeping bad providers and suppliers out of Medicare in the first place, and quickly removing wrongdoers from the program once they are detected. The twin pillar approach builds on CMS' use of the MACs, ZPICs, and RACs, and over time will leverage these contractor resources to more efficiently and effectively combat fraud, waste, and abuse and reduce improper payments.

The First Pillar: The Fraud Prevention System

CMS is committed to the goal of detecting potential fraud before suspect claims are paid. The FPS is the predictive analytic technology required under the Small Business Jobs Act. Since June 30, 2011, the FPS has been running predictive algorithms and other sophisticated analytics nationwide against all Medicare fee-for-service and Durable Medical Equipment, Prosthetics, Orthotics, and Supplies (DMEPOS) claims prior to payment and identifying automated claims edits that the MACs have then implemented. CMS is well ahead of the statutory implementation schedule, which called for phasing in the technology in the 10 highest fraud States in the Medicare fee-for-service program by July 1, 2011. Nationwide implementation of the technology maximizes the benefits of the FPS and permits CMS to efficiently integrate the technology into the Medicare fee-for-service program and train our anti-fraud contractors.

For the first time in the history of the program, CMS is using a system to apply advanced analytics against Medicare fee-for-service claims on a streaming, national basis. This system has enabled CMS to identify schemes operating across Medicare Parts A and B claims and across the country. The FPS aggregates Parts A and B claims in near-real time, and this comprehensive view of claims is revolutionizing our program integrity work. For example, ZPIC investigators formerly had to check multiple systems to determine whether a beneficiary ever visited the doctor who billed Medicare for services and supplies. The FPS has consolidated the dispersed pieces of potentially-related claims data – beneficiary visits with a doctor or orders for DMEPOS billed under Part B, and hospital and other provider services billed under Part A – enabling CMS and the ZPICs to automatically see the full picture. Equally important, the FPS organizes the data to quickly show when two providers or suppliers on opposite ends of the country are billing Medicare on behalf of the same beneficiary, rooting out potential compromised beneficiary numbers and other fraudulent activity.

Importantly, the FPS is a resource management tool; the system automatically sets priorities for our program integrity contractors' workload to target investigative resources to suspect claims and providers, and swiftly impose administrative action when warranted. The system generates alerts in order of priority, allowing program integrity analysts to further investigate the most egregious, suspect, or aberrant activity. CMS and our antifraud contractors use the FPS to stop, prevent, and identify improper payments using a variety of administrative tools and actions, including claim denials, payment suspensions, revocation of Medicare billing privileges, and referrals to law enforcement. The FPS is also strengthening CMS' ability to manage the ZPICs, for instance by permitting CMS to better observe and understand differences in how various ZPICs are managing similar issues.

In the first ten months of implementation of the FPS, the new preventive system resulted in:

- Leads for 591 new investigations
- Supporting information for 419 pre-existing investigations
- Leads for 550 direct interviews with providers and suppliers suspected of participating in fraudulent activity
- Leads for over 1,541 interviews with beneficiaries to confirm whether they received services for which the Medicare program had been billed.

The FPS may be compared to similar, more well-known predictive modeling technologies, such as the algorithms employed in the credit card industry to generate interviews of cardholders when suspect items are charged. Indeed the FPS metrics related to provider, supplier, and beneficiary interviews are particularly encouraging and exciting because they show that CMS has turned Congress' vision of bringing this proactive strategy to bear on a large scale in the Medicare arena into reality.

The Second Pillar: Enhanced Provider Enrollment and Automated Provider Screening

CMS must go beyond pay and chase to stop criminals whose intent is to enroll in Medicare, quickly submit a high dollar value of claims, and then close up shop once they have been paid. To prevent this from occurring, CMS has been working to strengthen upfront protections to keep bad actors out, as provider enrollment is the gateway to the Medicare program. This approach is more effective than one based solely on recovering overpayments because it is extremely difficult to recover overpayments from fraudulent providers and suppliers, whose goal is not to provide quality care to our beneficiaries, but rather to defraud taxpayers and CMS. Strengthened provider enrollment standards also protect beneficiaries from fraudulent providers who may provide inappropriate or low-quality care.

In September 2011, CMS began an ambitious project to revalidate the enrollment of all existing 1.5 million Medicare suppliers and providers by 2015 under the new Affordable Care Act screening requirements. The new requirements directed the Secretary to establish different levels of screening for categories of providers and suppliers based on risk. The three risk levels that have been established – limited, moderate, and high – correspond to increasing levels of scrutiny. Providers and suppliers in the moderate and high screening levels are subject to announced or unannounced site visits prior to either initial enrollment or revalidation. CMS has estimated that approximately 50,000 additional site visits will be conducted between March 2011 and March 2015 to ensure providers and suppliers are operational and meet certain enrollment requirements. Providers and suppliers in the high level of screening will be subject to new fingerprint-based criminal history checks after CMS awards a contract with an FBI-approved company in early 2013.

To complement the new screening requirements, CMS launched the Automated Provider Screening (APS) system on December 31, 2011. The MACs have historically relied on paper applications and crosschecking information manually against various databases to verify enrollment requirements such as licensure status. The APS conducts routine and automated screening checks of providers and suppliers against thousands of private and public databases to more efficiently identify and remove ineligible providers and suppliers from Medicare. CMS anticipates that the new process will decrease the application processing time for providers and suppliers, while enabling CMS to continuously monitor changes that may affect the accuracy of its enrollment data even after providers and suppliers are enrolled or revalidated, and to assess applicants' risk to the program using standard analyses of provider and supplier data.

Since March 25, 2011, CMS has enrolled or revalidated enrollment information for approximately 275,439 Medicare providers and suppliers under the enhanced screening requirements of the Affordable Care Act. The first phase of revalidation led to 13,066 deactivations of provider and supplier practice locations for non-response to the revalidation request, as of March 1, 2012. The second phase of revalidation has resulted in the deactivation of 6,278 provider and supplier enrollment records for non-response and 4,319 revocations after it was determined the providers and suppliers were not properly licensed in the State in which they were enrolled, as of May 1, 2012.[1]

Provider enrollment safeguards, recently improved by the new APS, are CMS's first line of defense against paying fraudulent or improper claims. These improvements are vitally important because they enable legitimate providers and suppliers to enroll easily and quickly in the Medicare program, while clamping down on bad actors to keep them out of the program.

Post-Payment Review and Recovery of Improper Payments

CMS has an additional opportunity to administratively recover improper payments after payment is made, through analysis and investigation conducted by Medicare contractors.

After payment is made, CMS and its contractors continue to analyze FPS results and historical claims data to identify suspected overpayments and potential fraud. ZPICs may make fraud referrals to law enforcement for further investigation, or identify and send potential fraudulent or improper payments to MACs to collect, or in some situations, do both.

In cases of fraud, CMS vigorously pursues post-payment remedies, including overpayment recoveries, in close collaboration with our law enforcement colleagues. In conjunction with CMS' antifraud efforts, our law enforcement partners have recovered $4.1 billion in FY 2011, including $2.5 billion to the Medicare Trust Fund. Our recovery efforts have been strengthened by collaboration between Department of Health and Human Services (HHS) and the Department of Justice (DOJ) on the joint Health Care Fraud Prevention & Enforcement Team (HEAT) which combines the agencies' analytic, investigative, and prosecutorial resources in fraud hot spots to form Strike Forces. Since 2008, the number of defendants charged with criminal health care fraud has increased by more than 75 percent, from 797 in 2008 to 1,430 in 2011.

For potential overpayment referrals to a MAC, the MAC makes a final determination as to the dollar amount to demand for recovery and sends the demand letter to the provider.

MACs validate ZPIC-recommended potential overpayments against a variety of sources, including contractual and regulatory requirements, as well as their review of the claims information. The MAC reviews the claims history to determine if there have been other adjustments or recovery actions, which could affect the demanded amount, and if the amounts identified were for claims paid within the past four years, the period that is open for collection of overpayment unless there is "fraud or similar fault." If there have been other adjustments or recovery actions on a claim, then the overpayment amount could be affected because portions of the ZPIC-identified overpayment may have already been recovered by the other Medicare contractors. While providers and suppliers may repay the overpaid amounts directly to a MAC, it is more typical for MACs to collect overpayments by adjusting future claims payments, making it operationally simple and effective to recoup payment from providers and suppliers that are still actively billing. If a provider or supplier appeals the determination, collection must be stayed until completion of the administrative appeals process. The provider or supplier has 120 days to appeal the overpayment determination. If providers or suppliers are delinquent on the repayment of determined overpayments after 6 months, the debt is referred to the Department of Treasury for collection.

While post-payment reviews may suffice to recover overpayments from legitimate, established providers and suppliers, there are significant challenges to recovering overpayments from those that are attempting to defraud the Medicare program. ZPICs target their analysis and investigative resources exclusively towards identifying possible illegitimate providers and fraud. However, MACs sometimes have difficulty recovering the ZPIC-identified overpayments since such illegitimate providers tend to close their businesses, liquidate their assets, or leave the country as soon as Medicare payments stop or when they receive an overpayment demand letter from the MACs. In these situations, the MACs' typical way of collecting overpayments by adjusting future claims may not be as effective, since there will be no future claims. Because of the nature of fraud and the fact that bad actors often are not operating legitimate, ongoing healthcare businesses, CMS' fraud prevention strategy is the key to protecting the Trust Funds from would-be bad actors. New tools available to CMS, like our twin pillar strategy, prevent payment to fraudsters in the first place and provide new ways to keep them from re-enrolling in some other guise, while working in conjunction with the aggressive pursuit of overpayment recoveries and support of our law enforcement partners in criminal investigations and prosecutions.

RACs conduct post-payment reviews and make recommendations to CMS by identifying opportunities for reducing improper payments. Overpayments identified by the Medicare FFS RACs are also sent to the MACs for collection. In the past, RAC reviews in Medicare have focused on incorrect coding, erroneous billing practices, and billing for the wrong setting of care. Unlike other Medicare program integrity contractors, RACs' reviews are more likely to identify overpayments from providers who are still enrolled and billing in Medicare.

The Medicare FFS RAC program has had increasing success since its national implementation in October 2009, which has resulted in the recovery of over $1.86 billion in overpayments. Already in the first half of FY 2012, the RACs have collected more overpayments than during all of FY 2011.

CMS MA AND PART D CONTRACTORS

The Medicare Advantage (MA) managed care benefit (Part C) and the prescription drug benefit (Part D) differ significantly from Medicare fee-for-service and, as a result, require different approaches and internal controls to measure and address improper payments. Unlike Medicare fee-for-service, CMS prospectively pays Medicare Part C and Part D plans a monthly capitated payment. Each per-person payment is based on a bid amount, approved by CMS, that reflects the plan's estimate of average costs to provide benefit coverage to enrollees. CMS adjusts these payments to take into account the cost associated with treating individual beneficiaries based on health status. This process is called "risk adjustment." CMS is using the Risk Adjustment Data Validation (RADV) program to reduce the payment error rate in the MA program and save taxpayer money. In addition, Part D payments are also reconciled against expected costs, and risk-sharing rules authorized in law are applied to further mitigate plan risk. All MA and Part C plans are required to have a compliance program in place, which includes a program to prevent, detect, and refer fraud, waste, and abuse. As part of these compliance program efforts, MA and Part D plans are also required to apply these policies and procedures to their downstream entities, such as their Pharmacy Benefit Manager, network pharmacies, and contracted providers.

CMS contracts with two private organizations, called Medicare Drug Integrity Contractors (MEDICs) for all MA and Part D program integrity work. The national benefit integrity MEDIC has the following responsibilities:

- Managing all incoming complaints about Part C and Part D fraud, waste, and abuse;
- Using new and innovative techniques to monitor and analyze information to help identify potential fraud;
- Working with law enforcement, MA and prescription drug plans, consumer groups, and other key partners to protect consumers and enforce Medicare's rules; and Identifying program vulnerabilities.

The outreach and education MEDIC has the following responsibilities:

- Facilitating a quarterly workgroup with key partners; and
- Providing basic tips for consumers on how to protect themselves from potential scams.

The national benefit integrity MEDIC also conducts proactive analyses that result in case referrals to law enforcement.

For example, the national benefit integrity MEDIC conducts a proactive analysis called Miles Too Great. Miles Too Great identifies instances when it is unlikely that a beneficiary could fill a prescription in two or more locations that are too far apart. This relatively simple calculation may identify drug-seeking beneficiaries, over-prescribers, or services not rendered.

Another method is to look at pharmacy change of ownership and determine if there is a sudden change in billing behavior after the change of ownership. From April 2010 to May 2012, the national benefit integrity MEDIC referred cases associated with $169 million in Part D payments to law enforcement because of proactive data analysis.

In FY 2011, the national benefit integrity MEDIC received approximately 342 actionable complaints (within the MEDIC's scope) per month, processed 34 requests for information from law enforcement per month, and referred an average of 36 cases per month. The national benefit integrity MEDIC was responsible for assisting the HHS Office of Inspector General and DOJ (through data analysis and investigative case development) in achieving 4 guilty pleas, 7 arrests, and 8 indictments. One case produced a 34-count indictment and included a group of 25 individuals and 26 pharmacies owned by one individual in the Detroit area involving approximately $38 million in Medicare funds.

The outreach and education MEDIC hosts quarterly Part C and Part D fraud workgroup meetings where attendees share information and data on identified or suspected fraudulent schemes.

CMS, pharmacy benefit managers, sponsoring organizations, MA plans, as well as local, State, and Federal law enforcement officials attended the workgroups. The Part D workgroup recently provided a useful forum for discussion of inventory shortages involving Part D claims (for example, drugs billed, but not dispensed).

Looking Forward

Medicare provides essential health benefits to millions of Americans who depend on the program to receive the health care they need. Protecting these benefits relies on coordination and communication between CMS and the contractors described today, as well as Medicare providers, beneficiaries, and law enforcement. CMS has demonstrated success in the collection of overpayments using the RACs, and I believe the new innovative, preventive antifraud tools will likewise provide increasingly greater program integrity protections to Medicare for a long time to come. CMS continues to implement a wide range of improvements aimed at preventing payments to bad actors that may not continue in business once their fraudulent activities are uncovered. Today, I am happy to say, CMS and our contractors have more tools than ever to implement strategic changes in pursuing and detecting fraud, waste, and abuse. I look forward to continuing to work with you as we make improvements in protecting the integrity of Federal health care programs and safeguarding taxpayer resources.

End Note

[1] We note that the first and second phase revalidation results are preliminary results as deactivated providers could reactivate over time with updated practice information or after showing evidence of proper licensing.

In: Fraud Detection and Deterrence ...
Editor: Anton Ferilli
ISBN: 978-1-62417-658-6

Chapter 5

TESTIMONY OF ROBERT A. VITO, REGIONAL INSPECTOR GENERAL, U.S. DEPARTMENT OF HEALTH AND HUMAN SERVICES. HEARING ON "MEDICARE CONTRACTORS' EFFORTS TO FIGHT FRAUD: MOVING BEYOND 'PAY AND CHASE'"*

Good morning Chairman Stearns, Ranking Member DeGette, and other distinguished Members of the Subcommittee. I am Robert Vito, Regional Inspector General for Evaluation and Inspections at the U.S. Department of Health and Human Services (HHS), Office of Inspector General (OIG). Thank you for the opportunity to testify about OIG's work on the fraud detection efforts of the Medicare benefit integrity contractors.

On June 28, 2001, OIG testified before this Subcommittee on performance problems that we had found in the fraud detection units at Medicare claims processing contractors. These problems included a lack of proactive case development, limited identification of program vulnerabilities, significant variation in the level of benefit integrity results across contractors, and a lack of uniformity and understanding of key fraud terms and definitions across contractors. A decade later, many of these same vulnerabilities regarding fraud

* This is an edited, reformatted and augmented version of testimony given on June 8, 2012, presented before the House Committee on Energy and Commerce, Subcommittee on Oversight and Investigations.

detection and preventions persist among the current benefit integrity contractors.

The Types of Medicare Benefit Integrity Contractors Have Changed but Similar Problems Persist

Types of Benefit Integrity Contractors

For more than a decade, OIG has been conducting reviews of the benefit integrity contractors that the Centers for Medicare & Medicaid Services (CMS) employs to reduce Medicare fraud, waste, and abuse. OIG began more than 15 years ago reviewing the anti-fraud and abuse activities conducted by the fraud units housed in the Medicare fiscal intermediaries and carriers.

In 1999, CMS began contracting with new entities called Program Safeguard Contactors (PSC) to detect and deter fraud in Medicare Parts A and B.[1] As a result of Medicare contracting reform required by the Medicare Prescription Drug, Improvement, and Modernization Act of 2003, CMS is currently replacing PSCs with Zone Program Integrity Contractors (ZPIC).[2]

With the inception of the Part D program, CMS contracted with Medicare Drug Integrity Contactors (MEDIC) to address potential fraud and abuse related to the Part D prescription drug benefit. In fiscal year 2007, CMS awarded contracts to three regional MEDICs. Since that time, all Part D benefit integrity activities have been assigned to a single MEDIC. This MEDIC also now has responsibility for detecting fraud in the entire Part C (i.e., Medicare Advantage) program.

Activities Performed by Benefit Integrity Contractors

CMS's benefit integrity contractors are generally tasked with:

- Proactively pursuing different sources and techniques for analyzing data to detect fraud.
- Conducting investigations to determine the facts and magnitude of alleged fraud and abuse cases.

- Referring cases of potential fraud to OIG or other law enforcement agencies.
- Assisting law enforcement by responding to requests for information.
- Identifying and reporting to CMS any systemic program vulnerabilities.
- Referring for collection any Medicare improper payments (i.e., overpayments) identified while conducting benefit integrity activities.

Problems Persist Regarding Benefit Integrity Contractors' Performance

Over the last 10 years there have been significant changes in both the number and types of contractors that CMS employs to protect Medicare from fraud, waste, and abuse. OIG reviews of these contractors have uncovered the following recurring issues that hinder the successful performance and oversight of the contractors, including:

- Limited results from proactive data analysis.
- Difficulties in obtaining the data needed to detect fraud.
- Inaccurate and inconsistent data reported by benefit integrity contractors.
- Limited use by CMS of contractor-reported fraud and abuse activity data in evaluating contractor performance and investigating variability across contractors.
- Lack of program vulnerability identification and resolution.

In addition, there is significant variance in the identification of overpayments among PSCs and only a small percentage of the overpayments referred by PSCs have been collected and returned to the Medicare program.

Benefit Integrity Contractors Have Had Limited Fraud Detection Results from Proactive Methods

Proactive data analysis has not represented a significant portion of benefit integrity contractors' activities. Instead, much of the benefit integrity contractors' fraud identification relies on reactive methods, such as complaints from external sources. The lack of proactive and early identification of fraud results in the Medicare program relying on the familiar "pay and chase" model rather than a risk reduction model that includes early detection and prevention of inappropriate payments.

As early as 1996, OIG began highlighting the limited nature of benefit integrity contractors' proactive approaches. In our first evaluations of the fiscal intermediary and carrier fraud units, OIG raised concerns about the lack of results from proactive methods.[3] In the case of fiscal intermediaries, half of the fraud units did not open any cases proactively.

PSCs were supposed to use innovative, proactive data analysis more than their predecessors, the claims processing fraud units. Yet, in OIG's review of PSCs in 2007, OIG found minimal results from proactive data analysis.[4] Thirteen of the 17 PSCs had less than 19 percent of their new investigations result from proactive data analysis. Two of these had no new investigations from proactive analysis.

As CMS has transitioned from PSCs to ZPICs, OIG has found that data provided to CMS by ZPICs about their fraud and abuse activities were not always accurate or uniform across contractors.[5] However, the two ZPICs reported an average of only 7 percent of new investigations coming from proactive methods.

Similarly in Medicare Part D, OIG has found that most incidents of potential fraud identified by the MEDICs came from external sources rather than proactive methods. OIG found that only 13 percent of Part D potential fraud incidents were identified through proactive methods.[6]

DIFFICULTIES IN ACCESSING DATA HAVE HINDERED BENEFIT INTEGRITY CONTRACTORS' ACTIVITIES

The current ZPICs and MEDICs' lack of access to Medicare claims data and, in the case of the MEDICs, medical records and prescriptions, has hindered or delayed their ability to fight fraud.

ZPICs reported that the lack of data access hindered their ability to identify potential fraud and abuse, respond to law enforcement requests for information, and track overpayment collections. At the start of their contracts, ZPICs had difficulties obtaining data. One ZPIC described difficulties obtaining claims data from a previous PSC and, therefore, decided to purchase the claims data on its own from another CMS contractor. Another ZPIC stated that the data necessary to fulfill requests for information were not available to them or had to be generated from multiple sources. ZPICs reported that improved data access would assist them in identifying potential fraud and abuse. Specifically, ZPICs indicated that having access to daily downloads of Medicare claims data would enable them to perform near-real-time analysis of provider and supplier billing activity. Early problems with accessing and using data also hindered MEDICs' ability to identify and investigate potential fraud and abuse. MEDICs reported that they need both Part D prescription drug event (PDE) data and Medicare Part B data to effectively identify and investigate instances of potential Part D fraud and abuse. However, CMS did not provide MEDICs with access to PDE data until August 2007, nearly a year after their contracts began. In addition, two MEDICs were not given access to Part B data until Fall 2008-2 years after their contracts began. Once they received access to PDE data, MEDICs reported that important variables were missing from the datasets or entered into incorrect data fields, making effective data analysis difficult.

Further, MEDICs' lack of authority to obtain information directly from pharmacies, pharmacy benefit managers, and physicians hindered their ability to investigate potential fraud and abuse incidents. MEDICs reported that because CMS contracts with plan sponsors, MEDICs have the authority to request information only from plan sponsors. Providing MEDICs with the authority to request information directly from providers and pharmacy benefit managers that provide Part D services could improve the efficiency and effectiveness of their fraud detection efforts.

OVERSIGHT OF CONTRACTOR PERFORMANCE IS LIMITED BY INACCURATE AND INCONSISTENT DATA AND BECAUSE CMS DOES NOT EVALUATE THE CAUSES OF VARIATION ACROSS CONTRACTORS

Inaccuracies and Inconsistencies in Contractor Performance Data Limit the Data's Usefulness

Benefit integrity contractors are required to report workload statistics related to their program integrity activities, including investigations and case referrals, periodically to CMS. However, OIG found that workload data used by CMS to oversee ZPICs were not accurate or uniform. This prevented OIG from making a conclusive assessment of their activities.[7]

The inaccuracies and the lack of uniformity in ZPIC data resulted from data system issues, ZPIC reporting errors, and ZPICs' differing interpretations of fraud terms and definitions. For example, the ZPICs counted and reported new investigations differently from each other in the workload statistics provided to CMS. Specifically, one ZPIC explained that it included all fraud complaints in its number of new investigations reported to CMS, regardless of whether those complaints were merged into one provider investigation. However, another ZPIC explained that if it received a complaint on a particular provider and started an investigation and then received another complaint on that provider, the subsequent complaint would not be counted as a new investigation in the workload statistics. This inconsistency could explain why one ZPIC reported seven times more investigations originating from external sources (e.g., complaints) than the other.

OIG has offered a number of recommendations to CMS about collecting a greater volume of benefit integrity results data, clarifying definitions of fraud terms and data definitions, and ensuring the validity and uniformity of this data. While CMS now requires benefit integrity contractors to report additional quantitative statistics, CMS still has not developed methods to ensure that all data provided by benefit integrity contractors is accurate and uniform.

CMS has not Assessed Differences in Performance Across Integrity Contractors

While one would expect that contractors would differ somewhat from one another in activity levels, OIG found significant differences in fraud detection activities across ZPICs (and in earlier work, across PSCs and fraud units). This variation could not always be explained by the size of the contractors' budget or oversight responsibility.

CMS has not systematically assessed the wide variation across contractors' activity data. In fact, CMS's contractor performance evaluations provide very few quantitative details about the contractors' achievements in detecting and deterring fraud and abuse.[8]

OIG has recommended that CMS perform more global assessments of performance across contractors; however, CMS has not performed these types of reviews. OIG continues to recommend that CMS review quantitative statistics across contractors to ensure that outlier data are investigated and to address the causes behind the variation in contractors' fraud detection levels.

Benefit Integrity Contractors Are Required to Report Medicare Program Vulnerabilities to CMS but Many Remain Unresolved

Medicare benefit integrity contractors are required to help prevent fraud, waste, and abuse by identifying systemic vulnerabilities in the Medicare program. However, OIG has found that some contractors are not reporting any program vulnerabilities to CMS. CMS defines program vulnerabilities as fraud, waste, or abuse identified through the analysis of Medicare data. Our early review of fraud units found that more than one-third of them had not identified any program vulnerabilities. In 2009, almost half of the benefit integrity contractors reviewed did not report any program vulnerabilities to CMS. The remaining PSCs, ZPICs, and MEDICs reported a total of 62 program vulnerabilities to CMS in 2009.[9] Further, although PSCs and ZPICs are required to report the monetary impact of vulnerabilities, these contractors reported impact for only 21 of the vulnerabilities. For the 21 vulnerabilities alone, the estimated monetary impact was $1.2 billion.

As of January 2011, CMS had not resolved or taken significant action on three-fourths of the 62 vulnerabilities reported in 2009. CMS took significant action to resolve 14 of the vulnerabilities, but only 2 of these had been fully resolved. OIG found that CMS lacked procedures to adequately track vulnerabilities and ensure that corrective actions are taken to resolve reported vulnerabilities.

Overpayments That Benefit Integrity Contractors Identified for Collection Did Not Result in Significant Medicare Recoveries

Benefit integrity contractors that are responsible for Medicare Parts A and B, i.e., the PSCs and ZPICs, are required to refer overpayments that they identify to the Medicare claims processors for collection. In response to a request from this Subcommittee, OIG issued a series of reports in 2010 concerning the identification and collection of Medicare overpayments referred by the PSCs for collection.[10] OIG found that only a very small percentage of overpayments that PSCs referred for collection was actually collected and returned to the Medicare program.

PSCs referred $835 million in overpayments to claim processors for collection in 2007. Similar to the variation found among benefit integrity contractors' fraud detection efforts, we found PSCs differed substantially in the amount of overpayments they referred for collection. Only two PSCs were responsible for 62 percent of the $835 million referred for collection by all PSCs.

Of the $835 million referred, only 7 percent, or $55 million, was collected by June 2008. The collection status for another 8 percent, or $64 million, could not be determined. For one out of every four overpayments referred by the PSCs, the claims processors reported that they did not receive the referrals or did not have any collection information.

Additional Corrective Actions Are Needed to Address Problems

OIG has recommended a number of corrective actions to address issues identified during our benefit integrity program reviews. CMS has implemented a number of these actions, but OIG continues to recommend the following additional actions to improve benefit integrity contractors' performance.

Oversee Proactive Identification of Fraud

If CMS expects ZPICs and MEDICs to continue to use proactive methods, CMS must ensure that this is being done effectively at each contactor.

Provide Timely Data Access

CMS must ensure that all contractors receive timely access to data especially during times of contractor transition. With regard to MEDICs' ability to directly access medical records and prescriptions, CMS should seek the authority to request medical records and information directly from the providers and pharmacy benefit managers that provide services for Part C Medicare Advantage and Part D prescription drug plans.

Improve Accuracy of Contractor-Reported Fraud Activity Data

CMS must develop methods to ensure that all data provided by benefit integrity contractors is accurate and uniform. CMS also needs to clearly define fraud and abuse terms that all contractor should use when reporting data.

Assess Variability in Performance Across Contractors

CMS should include more quantitative results in benefit integrity contractors' performance evaluations. Using both quantitative and qualitative data to describe achievements would provide a more comprehensive picture of contractor performance and provide CMS with valuable data for making contract renewal decisions. It would also allow CMS to conduct a more global assessment of performance across contractors. If uniform, quantitative results were included across contractors, CMS could investigate the causes of the significant variability of activity across contractors and the especially low volume of activity among certain contractors.

Ensure Program Vulnerability Identification and Resolution

To gain sufficient oversight of program vulnerabilities and reduce the risks to Medicare, CMS must have effective policies and procedures to (1) track vulnerabilities identified by all benefit integrity contractors, (2) ensure that all contractors are identifying and reporting vulnerabilities, and (3) ensure the prompt resolution of vulnerabilities.

Improve Overpayment Identification and Collection

CMS should develop effective procedures to ensure that PSCs, ZPICs, and claims processors are able to identify and track the collection status of all current and future overpayment referrals by benefit integrity contractors. CMS is responsible for ensuring that PSCs and ZPICs perform their overpayment identification effectively. To accomplish this, CMS must have complete and accurate information about overpayment referrals and the collection status of these referrals.

OIG Will Continue Reviewing Medicare Benefit Integrity Issues

With over $500 billion in Medicare benefit payments at risk each year, it is essential that all Medicare fraud-fighting partners do their utmost to ensure that fraud risks are minimized and program vulnerabilities are identified early and resolved quickly.

CMS is just beginning to employ its new twin pillars strategy for program integrity. The first pillar is the Fraud Prevention System (FPS). The FPS will utilize new contractors to perform predictive analytics that identify suspicious or inappropriate claims prior to payment. The second pillar is the Automated Provider Screening (APS) system, which identifies ineligible providers or suppliers prior to their enrollment or reenrollment.

As OIG did with prior strategies, we will review CMS's new strategy to determine its impact on reducing fraud and abuse in the Medicare program. OIG will begin reviews of the new enrollment procedures and the prepayment identification of inappropriate Medicare claims. OIG is also updating our previous work on MEDICs and will review how the current MEDIC has undertaken its new Part C fraud detection responsibilities. OIG is continuing to conduct evaluations regarding overpayments and Medicare debt collection. We are also conducting reviews to examine the activities of the Medicare Administrative Contractors and Recovery Audit Contractors.

Thank you for your support of OIG's mission and the opportunity to testify about benefit integrity contractors' fraud detection activities.

End Notes

[1] Through the years, some PSCs were given responsibility for both Parts A and B while others only Part A or Part B.

[2] With ZPICs, CMS intended to align all benefits in the Part A and B programs (including home health, hospice, and durable medical equipment) under a single ZPIC in each of seven geographic zones.

[3] OIG, *Carrier Fraud Units* (0E1-05-94-00470), November 1996 and *Fiscal Intermediary Fraud Units* (0E1-03-97-00350), November 1998.

[4] OIG, Medicare's *Program Safeguard Contractors: Activities to Detect and Deter Fraud and Abuse* (0E1-03-06-00010), July 2007.

[5] OIG, *Zone Program Integrity Contractors' Data Issues Hinder Effective Oversight* (0E1-03-09-00520), November 2011.

[6] OIG, *Medicare Drug Integrity Contractors' Identification of Potential Part D Fraud and Abuse* (0E1-03-08-00420), October 2009

[7] The lack of uniformity in ZPICs' reporting of data is similar to problems that OIG identified 15 years ago in its review of fiscal intermediary fraud units. In that review, OIG found that definitions of key fraud and abuse terms varied among CMS and its contractors, which hindered CMS's ability to interpret data and measure fraud unit performance.

[8] 01G, *Medicare's Program Safeguard Contractors: Performance Evaluation Reports* (0E1-03-04-00050), March 2006.

[9] OIG, *Addressing Vulnerabilities Reported by Medicare Benefit Integrity Contractors* (OH-03-10-00500), December 2011.

[10] OIG, *Medicare Overpayments Identified by Program Safeguard Contractors* (0E1-03-08-00031) and *Collection Status of Medicare Overpayments Identified by Program Safeguard Contractors* (0E1-03-08-0003) and *Collection Rate for Overpayments Made to Medicare Suppliers in South Florida* (0E1-03-09 00570), May 2010.

In: Fraud Detection and Deterrence …
Editor: Anton Ferilli

ISBN: 978-1-62417-658-6

Chapter 6

MEDICARE PROGRAM INTEGRITY: CMS CONTINUES EFFORTS TO STRENGTHEN THE SCREENING OF PROVIDERS AND SUPPLIERS*

United States Government Accountability Office

WHY GAO DID THIS STUDY

According to the Centers for Medicare & Medicaid Services (CMS)—the agency within the Department of Health and Human Services (HHS) that administers the Medicare program—more than 1.5 million health providers and suppliers of medical equipment were enrolled in the Medicare program in 2011, and 30,000 more enroll each month. CMS has established Medicare enrollment standards and procedures intended to ensure that only qualified providers and suppliers can enroll. While most providers and suppliers pose a limited risk to the Medicare program, our previous work found persistent weaknesses in CMS's Medicare enrollment standards and procedures that increased the risk of enrolling entities intent on defrauding the program. In 2010, the Patient Protection and Affordable Care Act (PPACA) authorized CMS to implement procedures to strengthen the Medicare enrollment process.

---

* This is an edited, reformatted and augmented version of United States Government Accountability Office Publication No. GAO-12-351, dated April 2012.

GAO was asked to review CMS's Medicare provider enrollment procedures. In this chapter, GAO describes (1) how CMS and its contractors use provider and supplier enrollment information to prevent improper payments and factors that may affect the usefulness of this information, and (2) the extent to which CMS has implemented new provider and supplier enrollment screening procedures since the enactment of PPACA. To do so, GAO reviewed relevant regulations and documents, and interviewed officials from CMS and a sample of four of the agency's contractors based on the volume of claims they processed and the status of their contracts with CMS.

What GAO Found

Medicare claims are screened against enrollment information, using automated enrollment-related prepayment edits, in an effort to prevent improper payments to ineligible providers and suppliers—such as those that are no longer active in the Medicare program or are not properly licensed to provide the services for which they have submitted claims. Officials with the contractors we interviewed described the use of several types of prepayment edits to ensure that claims data are valid. For example, verification edits are intended to check the provider's National Provider Identifier (NPI), which indicates whether the claim was submitted by an active provider or supplier. However, factors such as the frequency with which contractors have updated provider and supplier enrollment information and limitations of the data used may affect the timeliness and accuracy of data used to screen claims—in turn limiting the ability of the edits to prevent improper payments from occurring. For example, to update information maintained in the Provider Enrollment, Chain and Ownership System (PECOS)— CMS's centralized database for Medicare enrollment information—the contractors have relied on a variety of data sources that vary in the frequency with which they are updated and the ease with which the data can be accessed. We have previously reported concerns about the accuracy of the enrollment information in PECOS and recommended CMS increase its oversight of its contractors' provider and supplier enrollment activities. CMS acknowledged these concerns and indicated that the agency is working to address these issues.

Since the enactment of PPACA, CMS has implemented some new provider and supplier enrollment screening procedures and other measures intended to strengthen the existing Medicare enrollment process. New screening procedures include the designation of three different levels of risk of fraud, waste, and abuse, with categories of providers and suppliers assigned to limited, moderate, and high-risk levels—and those in the highest level subject to the most rigorous screening. For example, providers and suppliers in all three risk levels must undergo licensure checks, while those in moderate- and high-risk levels are subject to unannounced site visits. In addition, CMS implemented new application fees for some providers and suppliers. CMS also added two new Medicare contractors, an automated screening contractor and a site visit contractor, to conduct enhanced enrollment screening and site visits. CMS officials said that they expect the new automated screening contractor to identify additional data sources against which to screen, such as financial, tax, and business data sources. CMS's implementation of some additional enrollment screening procedures is still in progress. For example, by the end of 2012, CMS plans to contract with two Federal Bureau of Investigation-approved contractors to conduct fingerprint-based criminal background checks of high-risk providers and suppliers. In addition, the agency plans to extend the requirement for surety bonds to high-risk providers and suppliers beyond those already required of suppliers of durable medical equipment, orthotics and supplies. A surety bond guarantees that if a provider or supplier does not fulfill its obligation to Medicare, CMS can recover its losses via the surety bond.

HHS reviewed a draft of this chapter and in its written comments noted CMS's ongoing efforts to improve provider and supplier enrollment procedures. HHS also provided technical comments, which were incorporated as appropriate.

ABBREVIATIONS

A/B MAC	Medicare Administrative Contractor servicing both Part A and Part B lines of business
CHIP	State Children's Health Insurance Program
CMS	Centers for Medicare & Medicaid Services
CPI	Center for Program Integrity
DME	durable medical equipment
DMEPOS	durable medical equipment, prosthetics, orthotics, and supplies
DME MAC	Durable Medical Equipment Medicare Administrative Contractor
DMF	Death Master File

EDI	Electronic Data Interchange
EPLS	Excluded Parties List System
FBI	Federal Bureau of Investigation
FFS	fee-for-service
HHS	Department of Health and Human Services
HIPAA	Health Insurance Portability and Accountability Act
IRS	Internal Revenue Service
LEIE	List of Excluded Individuals/Entities
NPI	National Provider Identifier
NSC	National Supplier Clearinghouse
OIG	Office of Inspector General
PECOS	Provider Enrollment, Chain and Ownership System
PPACA	Patient Protection and Affordable Care Act
QASP	Quality Assurance Surveillance Plan
SSA	Social Security Administration

The Honorable Max Baucus
Chairman
Committee on Finance United States Senate

Dear Mr. Chairman:

For more than 20 years, we have designated Medicare as a high-risk program because of serious management challenges due to its size, complexity, and susceptibility to fraud, waste, abuse, and improper payments.[1] In 2011, Medicare covered 48.4 million individuals 65 years and older and eligible individuals with disabilities, and total Medicare program expenditures were $565 billion.[2] For fiscal year 2011, the Department of Health and Human Services (HHS) estimated the agency made improper payments of nearly $29 billion in the Medicare fee-forservice (FFS) program.[3]

More than 1.5 million health providers and suppliers of medical equipment were enrolled in the Medicare program in 2011, according to the Centers for Medicare & Medicaid Services (CMS)—the agency within HHS that administers the Medicare program—and 30,000 more enroll each month. CMS has established Medicare enrollment standards and procedures intended to ensure that only qualified providers and suppliers can enroll in the Medicare program.[4] For example, standards for suppliers of durable medical equipment, prosthetics, orthotics, and supplies (DMEPOS) include proper licensure and a physical facility on an appropriate site that is accessible to beneficiaries and

CMS. This information must be verified prior to enrollment.[5] Screening at the time of enrollment is a crucial step to reduce the risk of enrolling providers intent on defrauding or abusing the program.

According to CMS, the majority of providers and suppliers enrolling in Medicare are legitimate and pose a limited risk to the Medicare program. However, our previous work found persistent weaknesses in CMS's Medicare enrollment standards and procedures that increased the risk of enrolling entities intent on defrauding the Medicare program. For example, we found that the Medicare enrollment process for home health agencies did not routinely include verification of the criminal background of applicants, and without this information individuals and businesses that misrepresent their criminal backgrounds could be allowed to enroll in the Medicare program. 6 We also conducted covert testing and found that DMEPOS suppliers were enrolled who did not meet Medicare's standards or were not legitimate businesses.[7] We recommended stricter scrutiny of the enrollment processes for home health agencies and DMEPOS suppliers due to the higher incidence of improper payments among these providers. We also recommended strengthening Medicare enrollment standards and procedures as a key strategy for reducing fraud, waste, abuse, and improper payments in Medicare.

In 2010, the Congress passed the Patient Protection and Affordable Care Act (PPACA), which included provisions that will expand health insurance coverage to millions of individuals, and provided CMS with increased authority to combat fraud, waste, and abuse in Medicare. [8] Certain of these provisions are designed to strengthen Medicare's provider enrollment standards and procedures. For example, PPACA requires HHS to designate a level of screening according to the assessed risk of fraud, waste, and abuse with respect to the category of provider or supplier. At a minimum, PPACA requires all providers and suppliers to be subject to licensure checks, which may include checks in multiple states. PPACA gives CMS the authority to require additional screening procedures, such as criminal background checks, depending on the type of risk presented by the type of provider or supplier.[9]

CMS oversees a network of contractors that implement and monitor the Medicare program. Among these contractors are the Medicare Administrative Contractors (A/B MAC) that enroll and pay providers and suppliers, except for DMEPOS suppliers, for the services they provide to Medicare beneficiaries for Medicare Part A and Part B, the National Supplier Clearinghouse (NSC) that manages DMEPOS supplier enrollment, and the Durable Medical Equipment Medicare Administrative Contractors (DME MAC) that pay claims for DMEPOS items.[10] The A/B MACs also educate their enrolled providers and suppliers on CMS policies and procedures, provide information to beneficiaries, and undertake efforts to detect and prevent fraud and abuse. The NSC serves as the centralized contractor for the enrollment process and site visits for DMEPOS suppliers. In 2011, CMS awarded contracts to two new contractors—an automated screening and a national site visit contractor—to perform aspects of the provider and supplier enrollment screening process, including various screening activities and site visits beginning in 2012. Effective implementation by CMS of PPACA's provider and supplier enrollment provisions, through these and other contractors, is expected to aid CMS in its efforts to ensure that it only enrolls and pays providers and suppliers that meet Medicare's enrollment standards.

You asked us to examine how CMS uses enrollment information to prevent payment of improper or potentially fraudulent Medicare claims and to assess changes to CMS's Medicare provider enrollment procedures since the passage of PPACA. This chapter addresses (1) how CMS and its contractors use provider and supplier information to prevent improper payments and factors that may affect the usefulness of the enrollment information, and (2) the extent to which CMS has implemented new provider and supplier enrollment screening procedures since enactment of PPACA.

To assess how CMS and its contractors use provider and supplier enrollment information to prevent improper payments and factors that may affect the usefulness of the information, we obtained and reviewed: claims processing documents, including CMS procedural manuals and directives; claims processing schematics; and the criteria used to develop and implement prepayment edits that use enrollment information to ensure claims are only paid to providers and suppliers that are eligible to bill Medicare.[11] We examined the role of the data in the Provider Enrollment, Chain and Ownership System (PECOS) —CMS's centralized database for Medicare enrollment information—in the Medicare claims payment process. In addition, we reviewed our past reports and those issued by the HHS Office of Inspector General (HHS OIG) that discussed the accuracy of PECOS data.[12] We interviewed CMS officials and a total of four A/B and DME MACs on how they use provider and supplier enrollment information to prevent improper payments. We interviewed A/B MACs whose workloads were fully implemented by 2010 and whose contracts were not being recompeted during the course of our work.[13] In addition, we assessed A/B MAC claims processing workloads in order to select A/B MACs that had the largest percentages of the national workload. Our sample selection strategy resulted in two A/B MACs and two DME MACs.

To assess the extent to which CMS has implemented new provider and supplier enrollment screening procedures since the enactment of PPACA, we reviewed agency documents, including the Proposed and Final Rule that implemented PPACA's provider screening and other enrollment provisions, documents that described how PPACA-related enrollment processes compared to previous CMS enrollment procedures, and documents describing new processes that were not yet fully implemented. [14]We limited our review to only those PPACA provisions that establish provider and supplier enrollment conditions that must be met before enrollment in Medicare. We also interviewed CMS officials about provider and supplier enrollment screening procedures that were developed and implemented as a result of these PPACA provisions. In addition, we conducted interviews with the two A/B MACs to learn about their experiences implementing new enrollment procedures authorized by PPACA. We also interviewed NSC officials responsible for enrolling Medicare DMEPOS suppliers.

We conducted this performance audit from July 2011 to February 2012 in accordance with generally accepted government auditing standards. Those standards require that we plan and perform the audit to obtain sufficient, appropriate evidence to provide a reasonable basis for our findings and conclusions based on our audit objectives. We believe that the evidence obtained provides a reasonable basis for our findings and conclusions based on our audit objectives.

BACKGROUND

Medicare comprises 12 percent of the federal budget and is the third largest federal program after defense and Social Security. For fiscal year 2011, HHS reported an estimate of almost $29 billion in Medicare FFS improper payments. Our *Standards for Internal Control in the Federal Government* suggests that agencies should continually perform monitoring activities to reduce the incidence of improper payments.[15] However, our prior reports found weaknesses in CMS's monitoring of Medicare provider and supplier enrollment and claims payment contractors.[16] Partly in response to our work, CMS took steps to implement new DMEPOS supplier quality standards in an accreditation rule issued in August 2006 and proposed additional DMEPOS supplier enrollment standards in January 2008. To further address these concerns and create a focal point for all Medicare program integrity activities, in 2010, CMS established a Center for Program Integrity (CPI).[17] CPI, in collaboration with other components within CMS, develops and implements the agency's Medicare program integrity mission and goals. Among these goals is a reduction in instances of fraud, waste, and abuse, as well as strategies to ensure program vulnerabilities are identified and resolved.

According to CMS, the agency is pursuing an aggressive program integrity strategy to prevent payment of potentially fraudulent claims, rather than to recover funds from providers and suppliers after payment has already been made. Because identifying and prosecuting providers and suppliers engaged in potentially fraudulent activity is time consuming, resource intensive, and costly, CMS has designed measures intended to prevent enrollment by entities that might attempt to defraud or abuse the Medicare program. For example, the agency requires that applicants use a unique 10 digit National Provider Identifier (NPI) number and affirm that they are not excluded from participating in another federal health program. DMEPOS suppliers must also undergo pre-enrollment site visits. In addition, the agency requires enrollment information to be entered into PECOS, a single, centralized, provider and supplier enrollment database that assists with data sharing across the contractors' different geographic coverage areas. In addition, CMS has historically required the A/B MACs and the NSC to conduct activities, such as monthly reviews of state licensing board actions, to determine if individual providers continue to meet state licensing requirements and to conduct periodic checks to determine if entities continue to meet federal and state requirements for their respective provider or supplier type. With the implementation of the automated screening contract, these checks will be automated and conducted on a continuous basis, according to CMS.

Medicare Contractors

Since the Medicare program was created in 1965, it has been administered through a network of private contractors. CMS uses these contractors to conduct claims administration activities, to implement provider outreach and education, and to answer beneficiary inquiries through the 1-800-Medicare help line. Contractors also perform program integrity activities such as auditing providers and suppliers, reviewing claims for medical necessity, and conducting investigations of potential fraud, waste, and abuse. Central to program operations are the A/B MACs that manage Medicare provider and supplier enrollment, except for DMEPOS suppliers, and pay and review the claims submitted in their jurisdictions. In 2011, A/B MACs managed more than 1.5 million Medicare providers and suppliers. The previous year, A/B and DME MACs paid approximately 4.5 million claims each work day on behalf of CMS. Additionally, CMS contracts with the NSC to centralize the enrollment process and site visits for DMEPOS suppliers. In 2010, Medicare spent about $8.1 billion on DMEPOS supplies. In 2011, CMS added two new Medicare contractors to centralize and standardize the provider and supplier enrollment screening process.

Medicare Enrollment Process

To become eligible to bill for services or supplies provided to Medicare beneficiaries, providers and suppliers must apply to the program.[18] Entities applying to the Medicare program may complete an online enrollment form using PECOS or submit a paper application that is manually entered into PECOS by the A/B MACs or the NSC. Enrolling providers and suppliers submit identifying information such as their name, address, specialty area, and information about applicable licensure and accreditation.[19]

After the enrollment data are entered into PECOS, the A/B MACs and the NSC handle different aspects of the application process. The A/B MACs process all provider and supplier applications except for those for DMEPOS suppliers and the NSC processes all enrollment applications from DMEPOS suppliers nationally. Provider and supplier applications in PECOS are confirmed by the A/B MAC overseeing the jurisdiction where the services will be provided and by the NSC for DMEPOS suppliers. Contracts awarded in 2011 to new automated screening and site visit contractors altered this structure. CMS's new provider screening contractor will automate many of the required enrollment checks that the A/B MACs and the NSC have done manually and will allow CMS to monitor all providers and suppliers on a continuous basis to help ensure they continue to meet Medicare enrollment requirements. These contractors assumed some functions from the A/B MACS and the NSC in early 2012.

Prior to CMS's automated screening contractor assuming these responsibilities, the A/B MACs and the NSC confirmed the provider and supplier enrollment information by checking various data sources such as the Social Security Administration (SSA) to verify an individual's Social Security number, the National Plan and Provider Enumeration System to verify the provider's NPI, and state licensing boards to determine if the provider is appropriately licensed to furnish medical services within a given state. CMS also required the A/B MACs and the NSC to check additional data sources including the HHS OIG's List of Excluded Individuals/Entities[20] (LEIE) and the General Service Administration's Excluded Parties List System[21] (EPLS). Starting March 25, 2011, CMS required the A/B MACs to conduct site visits for categories of providers and suppliers designated as moderate and high risk. The NSC will continue to conduct site visits related to enrollment of DMEPOS suppliers. In addition, due to long-standing concerns about high rates of fraud, waste, and abuse by DMEPOS suppliers, they have been subject to additional enrollment requirements.[22] For example, DMEPOS suppliers must meet additional quality standards before they can be enrolled in Medicare, including proper accreditation, the successful completion of a site visit inspection, and posting of a $50,000 surety bond.[23]

Claims Processing and Enrollment-Related Prepayment Edits

CMS oversees contractors that manage the three major computer systems used to process Medicare Part A, Part B, and DMEPOS claims. Together, these computer systems are referred to as the "shared systems," because claims from all the A/B MACs and DME MACs are processed by these systems. CMS refers to the contractors that manage these systems as the "shared systems maintainers."[24] Provider and supplier enrollment information in PECOS is downloaded to the shared systems in provider files that are used in claims processing.[25] Information in the provider files is intended to ensure that providers and suppliers are eligible to receive payment for the services for which they have submitted claims. Although multiple contractors are involved in the claims payment process, the A/B and DME MACs are ultimately responsible for timely and accurate processing and payment of provider and supplier claims. For the relationship between the various contractors prior to January 2012 see figure 1.

Providers and suppliers submit most claims to Medicare electronically. Upon electronic submission, claims first pass through an Electronic Data Interchange (EDI) process that makes sure the claims are formatted using the nationally established standards to exchange electronic information between business entities.[26] In the EDI process, the claim is subject to automated prepayment controls called "edits." Here, front end edits screen the claim for formatting errors or missing data. For example, a front end edit checks the claim to ensure that it contains the required 10 digit NPI but would not check the validity of the NPI. Medicare contractors reported that Medicare Parts A and B and DMEPOS claims that do not pass front end edits are considered unprocessable and are returned by the contractors to the appropriate provider or supplier, which may then correct the error(s) and resubmit the claim.

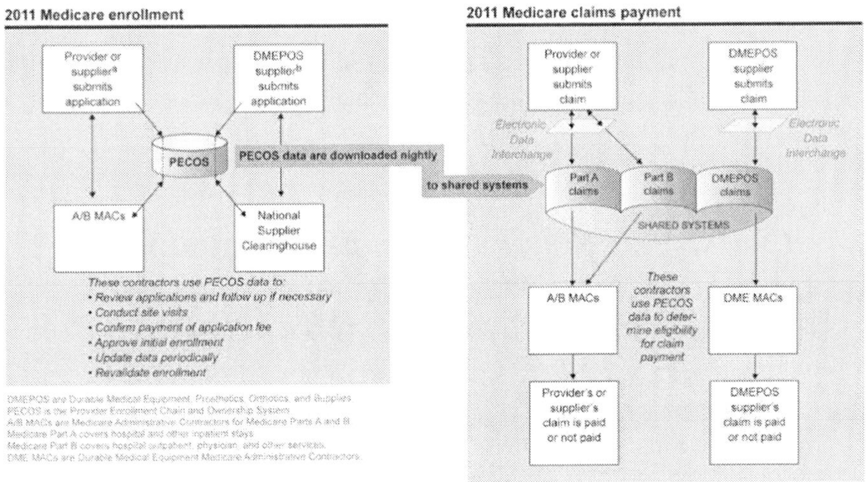

Source: GAO analysis of CMS data.

[a]Providers and suppliers include institutional providers such as hospitals and health care facilities, as well as physicians and nonphysician practitioners, who provide health care services to Medicare beneficiaries as well as certain Part B entities such as ambulance service providers, mammography centers, and portable X-ray facilities. The A/B MACS do not manage enrollment or claims processing for DMEPOS.

[b]DMEPOS suppliers include organizations that supply Medicare beneficiaries with durable medical equipment such as walkers and wheelchairs.

Figure 1. Medicare Enrollment and Claims Payment Process Prior to January 2012.

If a Medicare claim is in the correct electronic format and passes the front end edits, it is then sent for further processing in the shared systems. There, the claim is subject to a series of prepayment edits that can prevent payment of an incomplete or incorrect claim and may reduce improper payments and help minimize the extent to which the program is vulnerable to fraud, waste, and abuse. Prepayment edits include provider enrollment-related edits and subsequent edits that screen Medicare claims against other criteria, such as medical necessity.

Enrollment-related prepayment edits can be implemented on either the national or local level. The national enrollment-related prepayment edits are CMS-directed edits that are “hard coded” into the shared systems by the systems maintainers. National edits are updated quarterly and are standard across all A/B or DME MACs. In contrast, local prepayment edits are created and managed by the individual A/B or DME MACs. They may develop local enrollment-related prepayment edits based on differences in state law that determine the scope of a provider's or supplier's practice. CMS may also direct the A/B and DME MACs to develop local edits because they can be implemented on a more flexible schedule than CMS's quarterly updates to national edits.

CLAIMS ARE SCREENED AGAINST ENROLLMENT INFORMATION TO PREVENT IMPROPER PAYMENTS, BUT PREVENTION DEPENDS ON TIMELY AND ACCURATE INFORMATION

Medicare claims are screened during the payment process by a series of enrollment-related prepayment edits that check claims against provider and supplier information maintained in PECOS. Such edits are designed to prevent payments to providers and suppliers that the data indicate are ineligible to receive Medicare payment. While prepayment edits are in place to prevent improper payments, factors such as frequency of information updates and the limitations of the data used to update information in PECOS may affect the timeliness and accuracy of provider and supplier information. In turn, this may limit the extent to which enrollment-related edits prevent payments to ineligible providers and suppliers.

Enrollment-Related Prepayment Edits Are Designed to Prevent Payments to Ineligible Providers and Suppliers

Enrollment-related prepayment edits are designed to prevent payments to ineligible providers and suppliers—such as those that are no longer active in the Medicare program or that are not properly credentialed or licensed to provide the services for which they have submitted claims. Ineligible providers and suppliers may be enrolled in Medicare despite CMS's and its contractors' enrollment screening efforts. Officials with the A/B and DME MACs we interviewed described the application of prepayment edits to claims as a cascading series of checks that occurs progressively as the claim moves through the process according to the edits' "if/then" logic. For example, a certain edit will compare the NPI contained in a provider's file with the date of service contained in the claim, and if the NPI was active on the date of service, then the claim would move to the next stage of processing. The two types of enrollment-related prepayment edits are provider and supplier verification edits and specialty edits.

- **Provider and supplier verification prepayment edits**: Medicare claims are subject to edits that verify basic provider and supplier enrollment information. These enrollment-related verification edits screen the claim's data to ensure that the provider or supplier is eligible for payment. For example, such edits verify the validity of the entity's NPI, which indicates whether the claim was submitted by an active provider or supplier. Verification edits at this stage of claims processing also screen claims to ensure that the provider's or supplier's enrollment date is before the claim's date of service, thus indicating that they were an active provider or supplier on that date and therefore generally eligible for payment. A/B and DME MAC officials reported that claims failing these enrollment verification prepayment edits are not paid. Information on a denied claim due to provider or supplier ineligibility, including reason codes that explain the reason(s) for which the claim was not paid, is sent to the provider or supplier. These codes include reasons such as "the provider must update license information with the payer" and "invalid provider identifier." One DME MAC estimated that the number of claims denied due to the claim's date of service occurring outside of a DMEPOS supplier's "effective dates" for billing eligibility was only about 36,000 claims out of a total of about 50 million claims per year.
- **Specialty prepayment edits**: Enrollment-related specialty prepayment edits screen for provider- or item-specific information about providers or suppliers, such as their eligibility to bill for certain services that can only be provided by a certain provider type or specialty. For example, limited license providers such as chiropractors can only be paid for a limited number of allowable billing codes determined by CMS. Specialty edits screen claims to ensure that the claim contains these allowable codes. DME MAC officials told us that edits at this stage would also ensure, for example, that a podiatrist is only paid for podiatry services and not ophthalmology services.[27]

Verification and specialty enrollment-related prepayment edits may be implemented as either national or local edits. According to one A/B MAC we spoke with, because there is little differentiation among Part A providers most enrollment-related prepayment edits for these providers are implemented as national edits, which are programmed into the shared systems. A/B MAC officials reported that additional enrollment-related local edits are more likely to be implemented for Part B provider claims due to differences among states regarding reimbursement for certain services and provider types. These Part B specialty edits are implemented as local edits by the A/B MAC responsible for that state. Regarding DME claims, one contractor we spoke with reported that CMS more frequently standardizes the DME claims payment process. This assures uniform coverage decisions across all DME MACs. DME MAC officials reported that DME specialty edits include those applied to oxygen, pharmacy, prosthetics, and orthotics claims. For example, DME MAC officials told us that the edits applied to oxygen claims ensure that only suppliers who have the required valid license to provide oxygen services receive payment. All three types of claims—Part A, Part B, and DME—that fail prepayment edits, whether at the national or local level, are denied and returned to the provider or supplier with a reason code that explains why the claim was not paid. For example, it may indicate "this provider type/provider specialty may not bill this service."

While prepayment edits are implemented to reduce the likelihood of improper payments due to provider or supplier ineligibility, the effectiveness of specific enrollment-related edits is not assessed by the A/B or DME MACs or CMS. A/B MAC officials reported that they generally do not need to analyze data on claims that are not paid because a prepayment edit indicates the provider or supplier is ineligible to bill for services. Thus, these contractors do not report on which of the prepayment edits prevented the improper payment. A/B MAC officials explained that each enrollment-related prepayment edit is developed to perform a specific function and therefore they do not rank edits in order of their effectiveness in preventing improper payments. Additionally, they told us that they do not submit reports to CMS that identify which enrollment-related prepayment edits are most effective. CMS requires A/B MACs to submit quarterly supplements to monthly workload reports that provide the agency with information on the number of denied claims and reasons for denials, but this information is used to identify problem areas for resolution, measure trends in denial rates, and monitor fraud and abuse workloads. Although officials from one A/B and two DME MACs told us that they may generate reports on claim activity, these data generally are used for internal workload planning purposes or as the basis for provider education on proper coding, not to determine the effectiveness of certain categories of edits.[28]

Edits Depend on Timely and Accurate Information in PECOS

The ability of enrollment-related edits to prevent improper payments depends on the timeliness and accuracy of provider and supplier enrollment information contained in PECOS. In turn, the timeliness and accuracy of information in PECOS—which is downloaded as provider files into the shared systems each night—is affected by factors such as the frequency with which contractors update this information and limitations of the sources of the information used. A/B MACs and the NSC are responsible for updating PECOS when conducting initial and revalidation enrollment for providers and suppliers.[29] However, A/B MACs and the NSC were not able to confirm the status, such as licensure, of every provider or supplier in PECOS on a daily basis. Instead, certain aspects of provider and supplier status have been checked less frequently. For example, A/B MACs were required to conduct monthly reviews of provider licensure status and an A/B MAC official told us that they searched individual state websites for this information. A/B MACs and NSC also have relied on a variety of data sources such as state licensure boards, the HHS OIG's exclusions list, and SSA's Death Master File (DMF) to update provider and supplier information in PECOS. These sources vary in the ease with which A/B MACs and the NSC have been able to access their data and the frequency with which they are updated. For example, CMS officials reported that the A/B MACs had to manually access state data sources to update licensure status. In addition, contractors we spoke with said SSA releases updates to its DMF monthly and therefore there is an interval between a provider's death and when that information can be updated in PECOS. As a result, payments may still be made for claims submitted under a deceased provider's NPI for medical services allegedly provided after the provider's death. One A/B MAC official said that PECOS must first be updated to reflect the provider's status and this information in turn must be downloaded into the shared systems in a timely manner to prevent an improper payment from being made. This is because, while enrollment-related prepayment edits can identify and deny invalid claims, the edits use the existing provider and supplier information to do so. Thus, if the PECOS provider and supplier information is not current or is inaccurate, the edits will be ineffective in preventing improper payments.

We have previously reported concerns about the accuracy of the provider and supplier enrollment information in PECOS and CMS's oversight of A/B MACs' provider and supplier enrollment activities. CMS has acknowledged these concerns and indicated that the agency is working to address these issues. For example, we recently reported that incomplete or conflicting provider contact information in PECOS limited CMS from using its own data to operate its Physician Feedback Program.[30] Furthermore, in 2010 we reported that A/B MACs had difficulty recognizing when nursing home provider information in PECOS was incomplete or inaccurate and CMS oversight of A/B MACs in this regard was limited.[31] In that same report, we found that although CMS conducted desk reviews and onsite audits from years 2000 through 2009 to review contractors' management of nursing home providers' enrollment functions, these audits were limited. In addition, beyond these audits, CMS did not conduct checks on the PECOS database for internal consistency. According to a CMS official, this limited oversight was due to a lack of resources and competing priorities within the agency. As a result of these findings, we recommended that CMS more closely monitor the activities of A/B MACs' provider and supplier enrollment activities to help ensure the accuracy and completeness of PECOS data. CMS concurred with this recommendation and recently reported that the agency is evaluating the criteria it uses to assess A/B MACs' performance as it relates to the timeliness and accuracy of processing Medicare enrollment applications.[32] Further, the agency reported that it plans to evaluate the completeness and accuracy of provider and supplier enrollment data as part of reviews of the contractors' enrollment operations. Given that these activities have not been implemented, we could not determine their effect on the completeness and accuracy of PECOS data used to process claims or whether improper payments result from inaccurate information in the provider files.

CMS Has Implemented Some New Enrollment Screening Procedures Since PPACA, While Others Remain in Progress

Since the enactment of PPACA, CMS has implemented new provider and supplier enrollment screening procedures and has also implemented other measures intended to strengthen existing procedures. However, the implementation of some additional enrollment screening procedures by CMS is still in progress.

CMS Implemented Some New Screening Procedures and Added Measures Intended to Strengthen Other Existing Procedures

Since the enactment of PPACA, CMS has implemented some new provider and supplier enrollment screening procedures, and put in place other measures intended to strengthen existing procedures.[33] New screening procedures that define conditions for provider and supplier enrollment in Medicare include CMS's determination of different levels of screening according to the risk of fraud, waste, and abuse with respect to categories of providers or suppliers, and a new application fee for some types of providers. CMS also published a regulation consistent with its existing practice, requiring providers and suppliers to include their NPI on all enrollment applications and claims, and added two new Medicare contractors—an automated screening contractor and a site visit contractor—that are intended to conduct enhanced enrollment screening and site visits.

Provider and Supplier Risk Levels

To strengthen the screening activities already conducted by CMS's contractors, PPACA required that the level of screening applied to each category of provider and supplier be based on their assessed risk of fraud, waste, and abuse and that screening procedures for Medicare providers and suppliers be explicitly established. On February 2, 2011, CMS published a Final Rule to implement these new screening procedures. The Final Rule requires, among other things, that the A/B MACs and the NSC conduct enrollment screening based on categories of providers and suppliers and levels of risk.[34] CMS assigned these new risk levels—limited, moderate, and high—to categories of providers and suppliers based on determinations of which categories were at a greater risk for fraud, waste, and abuse. (See table 1.) A/B MACs and the NSC designate the appropriate screening level in PECOS for each enrolling provider and supplier upon submission of an application. Screening levels are designated based upon CMS guidance. As of October 2011, A/B MACs and the NSC had entered the screening level information in PECOS for all providers and suppliers that submitted an application.

Table 1. Categories of Medicare Providers and Suppliers Designated by Risk Level for Enrollment Screening

Risk level	Categories of Medicare providers and suppliers
Limited	Physician or nonphysician practitioners and medical groups or clinics, with the exception of physical therapists and physical therapy groups. Ambulatory surgical centers, competitive acquisition programs/Part B vendors, end-stage renal disease facilities, federally qualified health centers, histocompatibility laboratories,[a] hospitals, including criticalaccess hospitals, Indian Health Service facilities, mammography screening centers, mass immunization roster billers,[b] organ procurement organizations, pharmacies newly enrolling or revalidating, radiation therapy centers, religious nonmedical health care institutions, rural health clinics, and skilled nursing facilities.
Moderate	Ambulance suppliers, community mental health centers, comprehensive outpatient rehabilitation facilities, hospice organizations, independent diagnostic testing facilities, independent clinical laboratories, physical therapy including physical therapy groups, portable X-ray suppliers, and currently enrolled (revalidating) home health agencies.
High	Prospective (newly enrolling) home health agencies and prospective (newly enrolling) suppliers of durable medical equipment, prosthetics, orthotics, and supplies.

Source: GAO analysis of CMS Final Rule with Comment Period, Medicare, Medicaid, and Children's Health Insurance Programs: Additional Screening Requirements, Applications Fees, Temporary Enrollment Moratoria, Payment Suspensions and Compliance Plans for Providers and Suppliers, 76 Fed. Reg. 5862 (Feb. 2, 2011).

[a]The responsibility of the histocompatibility laboratory is to provide an evaluation of certain genetic data and pertinent patient immunologic risk factors that will allow the clinician and patient to decide which approaches to transplantation are in the patient's best interest.

[b]Mass immunization roster billers are providers and suppliers who enroll in the Medicare program to offer the influenza (flu) vaccinations to a large number of individuals, and they must be properly licensed in the states in which they plan to operate influenza clinics.

CMS stated that it assigned these categories of provider and supplier risk levels based on the agency's experience with claims data used to identify potentially fraudulent billing practices, as well as on the expertise of its contractors charged with investigating and identifying instances of Medicare fraud across providers and suppliers. The agency also based these risk levels on prior findings in reports by GAO and HHS OIG. In addition, CMS will adjust the screening level of an individual provider or supplier from "limited" or "moderate" to "high" based on other factors, such as whether the provider or supplier has had its Medicare billing privileges revoked, has been terminated or is otherwise precluded from billing Medicaid, or has been subject to any final adverse action within the past 10 years such as license revocation or suspension, or certain felony convictions.

Based on these new risk levels, providers and suppliers are subject to different screening procedures, with those in the high-risk level subject to the most rigorous screening. While PPACA requires that all categories of providers and suppliers be subject to licensure checks, it gave CMS discretion to establish a risk-based application of other screening procedures. CMS determined that providers and suppliers in all categories also must continue to undergo existing enrollment checks using various data sources to verify certain information such as Social Security number, NPI, HHS OIG exclusion, and taxpayer identification number.[35] According to CMS's new risk-based screening, moderate- and high-risk providers and suppliers additionally must undergo unscheduled or unannounced site visits, while high-risk providers and suppliers also will be subject to fingerprint-based criminal background checks.[36]

Application Fee

PPACA required HHS, for the first time, to impose an application fee on each institutional provider and on suppliers. In response, effective March 25, 2011, CMS, in its Final Rule, required all institutional providers and suppliers enrolling in Medicare, adding a practice location, or revalidating their enrollment to pay a $505 application fee.[37] PPACA specifies that amounts collected as the result of the application fee shall be used for program integrity efforts, including to cover the cost of enrollment screening and to carry out other screening.[38] However, PPACA permits CMS to grant a hardship exception for institutional providers and suppliers on a case-by-case basis if the agency determines that the imposition of the application fee would cause a hardship.[39] According to CMS officials, an institutional provider or supplier working with underserved populations or engaged in extensive charity work would be a possible candidate for a hardship exception. CMS has instructed its contractors in guidance on March 23, 2011, not to process any Medicare enrollment applications without the proper application fee having been paid or a hardship exception approved.[40] CMS transmits information about application fee payments by institutional providers and suppliers — which are made through an electronic payment system—to the A/B MACS or the NSC via PECOS.[41]

NPI Regulation

PPACA required HHS to promulgate a regulation for the inclusion of an NPI on all Medicare applications and claims by all providers and suppliers that qualify for an NPI—a practice that was already in effect.[42] The regulation was published as an interim Final Rule on May 5, 2010, and was effective July 6, 2010.[43] Prior to the PPACA requirement for a specific regulation, CMS had required contractors to confirm that providers and suppliers included their NPI on Medicare enrollment applications and claims. Since 2006, the agency has required that enrollment applications include an NPI and since 2008 providers and suppliers have been required to report their NPI on Medicare claims.[44]

New Screening and Site Visit Contractors

In a further effort to strengthen its enrollment processes, at the end of 2011, CMS contracted with an automated screening contractor to assume screening responsibilities from the A/B MACs and the NSC, and a site visit contractor to assume site visit responsibilities from the A/B MACs. CMS awarded a contract in September 2011 to an automated screening contractor that began screening new Medicare enrollments for all providers and suppliers, on December 31, 2011. Additionally, CMS officials said that the screening contractor was setting up baseline data and will assume the screening function for the A/B MACs and the NSC by the end of March 2012. The screening contractor will screen all providers and suppliers including DMEPOS suppliers. The automated screening contractor is responsible for electronically screening applicant information against various data sources used for enrollment to determine that the provider or supplier meets Medicare eligibility criteria such as valid licensure, accreditation, and a valid NPI, and is not on exclusion lists, such as the HHS OIG list of providers and suppliers excluded from participating in federally funded health care programs. This screening process results in a report to the A/B MACs and NSC that indicates the screening components that the applicant passed and also screening components flagged for additional review. The A/B MACs and NSC, which remain responsible for enrollment and revalidation, obtain documentation from the provider or supplier on any flagged information that requires additional review to determine if the applicant meets Medicare enrollment or revalidation requirements. In addition to conducting screening at enrollment and revalidation, the automated screening contractor conducts checks of certain screening information on an ongoing basis. For example, the automated screening contractor is responsible for validating licensure status at least weekly. Previously, A/B MACs and the NSC were responsible for manually reviewing state-provided licensure information monthly to determine if any enrolled Medicare providers' or suppliers' licenses had been revoked, suspended, or otherwise inactivated in the last 60 days.

CMS officials said that the automated screening contractor is developing an individual risk score for each provider or supplier. This individual risk score is similar to a credit risk score. The contractor's risk scores may be used eventually as additional risk criteria that determine screening activities for providers and suppliers.

CMS officials said the new automated screening contractor provides a centralized point for Medicare enrollment screening and allows for a national view of provider and supplier information, rather than the more limited regional view that the A/B MACs provided previously. For example, the automated screening contractor has been able to access information about providers and suppliers who operate across geographic regions. In addition, CMS officials said that the agency has taken a centralized approach to automated screening of enrollment data because of weaknesses observed in enrollment screening efforts, which were due generally to the large number of providers and suppliers for which the A/B MACs and the NSC had to manually screen applications and the lack of efficient access to data sources containing enrollment information. According to CMS officials, they expect the new automated screening contractor to improve the integrity of the enrollment and revalidation processes by automating the data checks and integrating new data sources. For example, CMS has directed the automated screening contractor to identify additional data sources for screening checks, such as financial, tax and business, and geospatial data sources.

Additionally, in December 2011, CMS contracted with a site visit contractor to perform nationwide physical site visits for all providers and suppliers, except DMEPOS suppliers, in the moderate- and high-risk screening categories in all states and six U.S. territories. The site visit contractor began conducting site visits and making site visit reports available electronically through a portal accessible to CMS and its other contractors in February 2012. These site visits previously were performed by the A/B MACs. The A/B MACs will order any required on-site visits through the site visit contractor, which will schedule and conduct them and provide the results to the appropriate A/B MAC. However, the NSC will continue to conduct site visits related to provider enrollment of DMEPOS suppliers.[45]

CMS requires two types of site visits: routine and rapid response. According to CMS, routine site visits involve a physical location verification and collection of required data elements using predefined checklists. Rapid response site visits are triggered by an alert of possible fraudulent activity, and may require the same elements as a routine site visit but with rapid reporting and response due to the alert. Except for DMEPOS suppliers, the national site visit contractor collects site visit information at the physical provider or supplier site using defined questionnaires and gathers photographic evidence for transmission to CMS. The data elements required during routine and rapid response site visits include validation of the physical location of the provider or supplier, including capturing global positioning system coordinates of the site, photographs of the door of the provider or supplier office, and signage of the office. The contractor is required to conduct site visits and deliver completed site visit reports within a specified time period. Depending on the request from CMS or an A/B MAC, the contractor will make site visits within 30, 15, or 7 days, for routine visits, or within 36 hours for rapid response visits. CMS estimated that in the first year of the contract, the site visit contractor would conduct nearly 60,000 site visits within 30 days, almost 5,000 site visits within 15 days, almost 1,000 site visits within 7 days, and about 30 rapid response site visits. CMS officials said the national site visit contractor is expected to provide consistency of site visits across the country and, similar to the automated screening contractor, reduce the A/B MACs' workloads.

Several New Screening Procedures Remain in Progress

CMS's implementation of some enrollment screening procedures authorized by PPACA remains in progress, including efforts to (1) extend surety bond requirements to additional providers and suppliers, (2) conduct fingerprint-based criminal background checks of high-risk providers and suppliers, (3) require enrolling providers and suppliers to disclose additional types of information, and (4) require compliance and ethics programs for providers and suppliers.

Extend Surety Bond Requirements to Additional Providers and Suppliers

CMS is in the process of drafting a proposed rule to extend the surety bond requirement to certain providers and other suppliers.[46] Previously, surety bonds generally had been required only for DMEPOS suppliers.[47] Specifically, CMS officials said that they are seeking comments on extending surety bonds to home health agencies and independent diagnostic testing facilities (and, potentially, outpatient rehabilitation facilities) and that they expected to issue a proposed rule to require surety bonds as conditions of enrollment for certain other types of providers in the fall of 2012. PPACA extended CMS's authority to impose surety bonds on certain additional providers and suppliers, based on a determination about their level of risk.[48] The surety bond would be in an amount commensurate with the provider's or supplier's billing volume, but not less than $50,000. CMS officials also said they are considering giving a new supplier provisional enrollment and then setting the amount of the surety bond after a review of billing activities.

While CMS is considering extending surety bonds to additional providers and suppliers, a 2011 HHS OIG report stated that CMS did not have finalized procedures for recovering DMEPOS overpayments through surety bonds, and therefore, as of July 2011, no overpayments had been recovered through surety bonds since October 2, 2009, the date the surety bond requirement became effective.[49] However, in January 2012, CMS released guidance on claims against surety bonds for DMEPOS suppliers.[50] The guidance states that the surety—a company that provides the surety bond —is liable for any overpayments incurred during the term of the surety bond and that the surety must pay CMS within 30 days of receiving written notice of an overpayment. CMS's guidance also advises DME MACs on how to collect overpayments incurred during the term of a surety bond. CMS officials said that they expect that many of the requirements for obtaining and maintaining DMEPOS surety bonds can be easily applied to home health agencies and independent diagnostic testing facilities.

Conduct Fingerprint-Based Criminal Background Checks of High-Risk Providers and Suppliers

CMS officials said the agency was working with the Federal Bureau of Investigation (FBI) to gain access to its criminal background information for use in conducting fingerprint-based criminal background checks of high-risk providers and suppliers. PPACA authorized, but did not require, the use of criminal background checks in its risk-based provider and supplier screening. In order to conduct criminal background checks, CMS officials said they will contract with FBI channelers, whose contracts were recently recompeted by the FBI; CMS officials said that as of December 2011, 20 contracts were approved and 13 had been awarded by the FBI.[51] CMS plans to contract with two channelers, one to conduct background checks and one to handle provider and supplier fingerprinting. CMS officials said they are developing a scope of work to solicit among the FBI-approved channelers and expect to have contracts in place before the end of 2012. CMS officials also said that they plan to develop guidance to further define A/B MAC and NSC responsibilities and work flow of these checks.

Requiring Providers and Suppliers to Disclose Additional Information

CMS officials said the agency was developing and reviewing regulations to address the requirement for increased disclosures for enrolling or revalidating Medicare providers and suppliers. PPACA requires providers and suppliers to disclose any current or previous affiliation with another provider or supplier that has uncollected debt; has been or is subject to a payment suspension under a federal health care program; has been excluded from participation under Medicare, Medicaid, or CHIP; or has had its billing privileges denied or revoked at the time of initial enrollment or revalidation of enrollment. CMS officials noted that the development of these regulations is complicated by many issues that need to be addressed, such as provider and supplier concern about what information will be collected, what CMS will do with information once it is collected, and how to address concerns about maintaining the privacy and security of the information. CMS officials said the agency did not meet its own time frame for publishing a regulation to address this PPACA provision by November 2011 and they are not certain when the regulation will be published.

Development of Regulations for a Compliance and Ethics Program

CMS officials said that the agency was studying criteria found in HHS OIG model plans as it worked to address the PPACA requirement that the agency establish the core elements of compliance and ethics programs for providers and suppliers. PPACA required that Medicare providers establish compliance programs that contain the core elements established by CMS in consultation with the HHS OIG. In general, a compliance program is the internal set of policies, processes, and procedures that a provider organization implements to help it act ethically and lawfully. In this context, a compliance program is intended to help provider and supplier organizations prevent and detect violations of Medicare laws and regulations. CMS does not have a projected target date for implementation.

CONCLUSION

Timely and accurate Medicare provider and supplier enrollment information maintained in the PECOS database are essential to reducing fraud, waste, and abuse and the likelihood of making improper payments. Although PECOS information has been routinely updated by CMS's A/B MACs and the NSC using multiple national and state data sources, limitations in these data sources and in the frequency with which updates are made may lead to delays in, or failures to, accurately update information in PECOS, resulting in payments to ineligible providers or suppliers. As a result of the provisions in PPACA, CMS has begun to supplement its previous provider enrollment activities with new procedures and contracts that have the potential to improve the accuracy and timeliness of information stored in PECOS. In particular, CMS's new enrollment screening and site visit contracts shift some provider enrollment activities from the A/B MACs and NSC to centralized national contractors. CMS anticipates that the new screening contractor will improve the accuracy and timeliness of updates to the provider enrollment information in PECOS by automating the process and using additional data sources for enrollment screening. In addition, CMS expects that the new site visit contractor will enable the agency to conduct routine and targeted site visits of certain providers and suppliers in categories considered at greater risk for submitting improper or potentially fraudulent Medicare claims. Our previous work has found, and we recommended, that contractor monitoring is needed to ensure that CMS and its contractors identify and address the causes of improper payments. However, it is too early to determine whether these new contractors—and the agency's pending action on other PPACA provisions intended to strengthen provider enrollment standards—will improve the integrity of the Medicare provider enrollment and claims payment processes and reduce the likelihood of improper payments.

AGENCY COMMENTS

HHS reviewed a draft of this chapter and in its written comments highlighted continuing steps that CMS is taking to improve the accuracy and timeliness of data used to screen providers and suppliers and to further strengthen contractor oversight and PECOS data integrity. In its general comments, HHS noted that, since we conducted our work, CMS has increased the frequency with which it receives the SSA's DMF and now populates PECOS with this information weekly, rather than monthly. In addition, CMS will use its new automated screening contractor to routinely monitor changes that can affect enrollment status, such as death or loss of required licenses for providers and suppliers. HHS also commented that CMS is taking action to further strengthen quality control by performing follow-up analysis to ensure actions reported during the enrollment and revalidation processes are properly updated in PECOS. HHS noted that CMS is taking steps to improve the QASP process used to evaluate specific contractor functions by improving the depth at which these studies are performed and concentrating on areas that affect the quality of PECOS data. HHS also provided technical comments, which we incorporated as appropriate.

Sincerely yours,

Kathleen M. King
Director, Health Care

End Notes

[1] Fraud represents intentional acts of deception with knowledge that the action or representation could result in an inappropriate gain. Waste includes inaccurate payments for services, such as unintentional duplicate payments. Abuse represents actions inconsistent with acceptable business or medical practices. An improper payment is any payment that should not have been made or that was made in an incorrect amount (including overpayments and underpayments) under statutory, contractual, administrative, or other legally applicable requirements. In 1990, we began to report on government operations that we identified as "high risk" for serious weaknesses in areas that involve substantial resources and provide critical services to the public. See GAO, *High-Risk Series: An Update*, GAO-11-278 (Washington, D.C.: February 2011).

[2] Medicare consists of four parts. Medicare Part A covers inpatient hospital care, skilled nursing facility care, some home health care services, and hospice care. Part B services include physician and outpatient hospital services, diagnostic tests, mental health services, outpatient physical and occupational therapy, ambulance services, prosthetics, orthotics, and supplies. Medicare Parts A and B are known as original Medicare or Medicare Fee-for-Service (FFS). CMS also contracts with private health plans to administer a Medicare private plan, known as Medicare Part C or Medicare Advantage, and drug plan sponsors to administer the Medicare outpatient prescription drug benefit known as Medicare Part D.

[3] HHS, *Fiscal Year 2011 Agency Financial Report* (Washington, D.C.: Nov. 15, 2011).

[4] The term provider refers collectively to institutional providers such as hospitals, and health care facilities, as well as physicians and nonphysician practitioners who provide health care services to Medicare beneficiaries. Providers also include organ procurement organizations, skilled nursing facilities, hospice, and end-stage renal disease centers. The term suppliers refers to certain Part B entities such as ambulance service providers, mammography centers, and portable X-ray facilities. Suppliers also include entities that supply Medicare beneficiaries with durable medical equipment, prosthetics, orthotics, and supplies (DMEPOS) such as walkers and wheelchairs. Medicare law defines durable medical equipment (DME) as equipment that serves a medical purpose, can withstand repeated use,

is generally not useful in the absence of an illness or injury, and is appropriate for use in the home. This chapter will use the term providers and suppliers when referring to all Medicare providers and suppliers but will specify DMEPOS suppliers when necessary.

[5] Enrolling in Medicare enables providers or suppliers to submit claims for services and supplies provided to Medicare beneficiaries.

[6] See GAO, *Medicare: Improvements Needed to Address Improper Payments in Home Health,* GAO-09-185 (Washington, D.C.: Feb. 27, 2009).

[7] See GAO, *Medicare: Covert Testing Exposes Weaknesses in the Durable Medical Equipment Supplier Screening Process*, GAO-08-955 (Washington, D.C.: July 3, 2008).

[8] Pub. L. No. 111-148, 124 Stat. 119 (2010), as amended by the Health Care and Education Reconciliation Act of 2010 (HCERA), Pub. L. No. 111-152, 124 Stat. 1029, which we refer to collectively as PPACA.

[9] PPACA, § 6401, 124 Stat. 119, 747-753, amended by § 10603, 124 Stat. 119. 1006 (codified at 42 U.S.C. § 1395cc(j)).

[10] CMS currently contracts with 10 A/B MACs that are responsible for their own geographic regions, known as jurisdictions. A total of 14 jurisdictions now exist and future consolidations will bring the total to 10 jurisdictions. There are four DME MACs that process claims for DMEPOS supplies.

[11] We did not assess prepayment edits based on CMS policies on coverage of medical care or medical necessity.

[12] Due to CMS's recent implementation of agreements with new contractors to manage certain aspects of the Medicare provider enrollment process, we did not assess whether these contractors will improve the accuracy of the data in PECOS.

[13] In response to contracting reform requirements in the Medicare Prescription Drug, Improvement, and Modernization Act of 2003, CMS has been transitioning its claims processing contracts from 51 contractors to no more than 10 MACs that will process Medicare Part A and Part B provider and supplier enrollment applications and pay claims, except for DMEPOS enrollment and claims. Due to this consolidation and transitioning of workloads between contractors, we avoided selecting MACs that could have lost their contracts during the course of our engagement.

[14] *Medicare, Medicaid, and Children's Health Insurance Programs; Additional Screening Requirements, Application Fees, Temporary Enrollment Moratoria, Payment Suspensions and Compliance Plans for Providers and Suppliers*, 76 Fed. Reg. 5862 (Feb. 2, 2011).

[15] GAO, *Standards for Internal Control in the Federal Government*, GAO/AIMD-00-21.3.1 (Washington, D.C.: November 1999). Internal controls are components of an organization's management that provide reasonable assurances that certain objectives, including effectiveness and efficiency of operations, are being achieved.

[16] See GAO, *Medicare: CMS's Program Safeguards Did Not Deter Growth in Spending for Power Wheelchairs*, GAO-05-43 (Washington, D.C.: Nov. 17, 2004), *Medicare: More Effective Screening and Stronger Enrollment Standards Needed for Medical Equipment Suppliers*, GAO-05-656 (Washington, D.C.: Sept. 22, 2005), *Medicare: Improvements Needed to Address Improper Payments for Medical Equipment and Supplies*, GAO-07-59 (Washington, D.C.: Jan. 31, 2007), *Medicare: Improvements Needed to Address Improper Payments in Home Health*, GAO-09-185 (Washington, D.C.: Feb. 27, 2009), and *Medicare Contracting Reform: Agency Has Made Progress with Implementation, but Contractors Have Not Met All Performance Standards*, GAO-10-71 (Washington, D.C.: Mar. 25, 2010).

[17] CPI also coordinates CMS's program integrity efforts for Medicaid and the Children's Health Insurance Program.

[18] To remain eligible for payment, providers and suppliers must continue to meet CMS's Medicare enrollment requirements and periodically revalidate their enrollment information with the A/B MACs or the NSC.

[19] Licensure is a mandatory process by which a state government grants permission to an individual practitioner or health care organization to engage in an occupation or profession. Accreditation is a formal process by which a recognized body, usually a nongovernmental organization, assesses and recognizes that a health care organization meets applicable predetermined standards. Whereas licensure is a mandatory process, accreditation is usually voluntary although CMS requires accreditation as a condition for suppliers enrolling in Medicare. Some of the other required enrollment information includes: an agreement for electronic funds transfer, a Social Security or tax identification number, name of medical or professional school and year graduated, or residency status.

[20] The OIG's LEIE includes all individuals and entities currently excluded from participating in federally funded health care programs including Medicare and Medicaid. Exclusions are imposed for a number of reasons including: (1) Medicare or Medicaid fraud, as well as any other offenses related to the delivery of items or services under Medicare, Medicaid, CHIP, or other State health care programs; (2) patient abuse or neglect; (3) felony convictions for other health care-related fraud, theft, or other financial misconduct; and (4) felony convictions relating to unlawful manufacture, distribution, prescription, or dispensing of controlled substances.

[21] The EPLS includes information on entities debarred, suspended, proposed for debarment, excluded, or disqualified by federal government agencies from receiving federal contracts or federally approved subcontracts and from certain types of federal financial and nonfinancial assistance and benefits.

[22] The Medicare Prescription Drug Improvement and Modernization Act required the Secretary to establish and implement quality standards for DMEPOS suppliers. Pub. L. No. 108-173, § 302, 117 Stat. 2066, 2223 (Dec. 8, 2003).

[23] A surety bond is a bond issued by an entity guaranteeing that a provider or supplier will fulfill its obligation to Medicare. If the obligation is not met, CMS is required to recover its losses via the surety bond. DMEPOS suppliers are required to obtain and submit a bond of no less than $50,000 for each NPI that is assigned by CMS. Because DMEPOS suppliers must obtain an NPI by practice location, a DMEPOS supplier with 20 practice locations would be required to secure a $1 million surety bond.

[24] System maintenance includes activities such as programming software changes needed to correct errors or to implement functionality through "hard coded" edits.

[25] Although the A/B and DME MACs we interviewed referred to it as a provider file, it also includes enrollment information on suppliers.

[26] The Health Insurance Portability and Accountability Act (HIPAA) mandated that covered entities in the health care industry use standard formats for electronic claims and claims-related transactions. 42 U.S.C. § 1320d-2. CMS's EDI includes two systems—the Common Edits and Enhancements module and the Common Electronic Data Interchange—that are used for Medicare Part A and Part B claims and DMEPOS claims, respectively. Paper claims are put into electronic format for processing.

[27] Medicare claims also undergo prepayment edits that are not related to provider enrollment information. Examples include edits that screen for excessive units of service— known as medically unlikely edits—and compliance with Medicare coverage policies.

[28] For example, A/B MACs indicated that many provider-related claim denials are due to providers submitting claims for dates of service outside of the provider's eligibility dates.

[29] PPACA requires all existing provider and supplier information to be revalidated by 2015. PPACA, § 6401, 124 Stat. 119, 749, amended by § 10603, 124 Stat. 119. 1006 (codified at 42 U.S.C. § 1395cc(j)). After the revalidation of all providers and suppliers required by PPACA, CMS's current cycle for revalidation—3 years for DMEPOS suppliers and 5 years for all other providers and suppliers—will apply. CMS retains the authority to require a provider or supplier to revalidate off-cycle when certain compliance-related concerns arise. PECOS data must also be updated when there is a change of address or other change to provider or supplier status.

[30] The Medicare Improvements for Patients and Providers Act of 2008 (MIPPA) required HHS to establish and begin implementing by January 1, 2009, a Physician Feedback Program that would include distribution of confidential feedback reports to physicians on the resources used to provide care to Medicare beneficiaries. Pub. L. No. 110-275, § 131, 122 Stat. 2492, 2526-2527 (July 15, 2008). See GAO, *Medicare Physician Feedback Program: CMS Faces Challenges with Methodology and Distribution of Physician Reports,* GAO-11-720 (Washington, D.C.: Aug. 12, 2011).

[31] See GAO, *Nursing Homes: Complexity of Private Investment Purchases Demonstrates Need for CMS to Improve the Usability and Completeness of Ownership Data,* GAO-10-710 (Washington, D.C.: Sept. 30, 2010).

[32] CMS uses its Quality Assurance Surveillance Plans (QASP) to evaluate A/B and DME MAC's fulfillment of contract requirements. The QASP describes CMS's plan for inspecting the work within the various business functions that the MACs conduct.

[33] PPACA also applies to certain enrollment provisions related to Medicaid or to the state Children's Health Insurance Program (CHIP). Medicaid is the federal-state program that covers acute health care, long-term care, and other services for low-income people. CHIP is the joint federal-state program that provides health coverage to children whose families have incomes that are low, but not low enough to qualify for Medicaid. This chapter does not discuss how PPACA affects either Medicaid or CHIP.

[34] *Medicare, Medicaid, and Children's Health Insurance Programs; Additional Screening Requirements, Application Fees, Temporary Enrollment Moratoria, Payment Suspensions and Compliance Plans for Providers and Suppliers,* 76 Fed. Reg. 5862 (Feb. 2, 2011).

[35] A taxpayer identification number is an identification number used by the Internal Revenue Service (IRS) in the administration of tax laws. It is issued either by the SSA or by the IRS.

[36] All individuals with a direct or indirect ownership interest of 5 percent or greater in high-risk providers and suppliers are subject to fingerprint-based criminal background checks.

[37] Institutional providers include hospitals, home health agencies, community mental health centers, and skilled nursing facilities. Application fees do not apply to physicians, nonphysician practitioners, physician organizations, and nonphysician organizations. Suppliers include DMEPOS suppliers and other suppliers including ambulance service providers, mammography centers, and independent clinical laboratories.

[38] PPACA, § 6401, 124 Stat. 119, 748, amended by § 10603, 124 Stat. 119. 1006 (codified at 42 U.S.C. § 1395cc(j)). PPACA established that fee amounts for subsequent years would be equal to the preceding year's fee adjusted by the percentage change in the Consumer Price Index (for all urban consumers) for the 12-month period ending on June 30 of the prior year.

[39] CMS stated that a provider or supplier requesting a hardship exception must submit documentation of the need for an exception. For example, the application must include a letter and supporting documentation that describe the significant burden and why it merits an exception.

[40] A/B MACs and the NSC must notify a provider or supplier who does not submit a fee or hardship exception request that it has 30 days from the date of the letter to pay the application fee, and that failure to do so will result in the rejection of the enrollment application (for initial enrollments and new practice locations) or revocation of the provider's Medicare billing privileges (for revalidation). The letter must also state that because a hardship exemption request was not submitted with the original application, such a request will not be considered in lieu of the fee. If the fee is paid within the 30 day period, the contractor may begin processing the application.

[41] The provider or supplier must pay the application fee electronically through http://www.pay.gov. Pay.gov is the federal government website where individuals can submit payment to various federal agencies on-line.

[42] PPACA, § 6402, 124 Stat. 119, 753-763 (codified at 42 U.S.C. § 1320a-7k).

[43] *Medicare and Medicaid Programs; Changes in Provider and Supplier Enrollment, Ordering and Referring, and Documentation Requirements, and Changes in Provider Agreements,* 75 Fed. Reg. 24437 (May 5, 2010).

[44] HIPAA required that HHS adopt standards for unique health identifiers. In a Final Rule, CMS adopted the NPI as the standard unique health identifier for health care providers. *Centers for Medicare & Medicaid Services, The National Provider Identifier Rule*, 69 Fed. Reg. 3434 (Jan. 23, 2004). Consistent with the NPI Final Rule, beginning in 2006, the Medicare program required providers and suppliers to report their NPIs on their enrollment applications.

[45] CMS at times exercises its authority to conduct a site visit or request its contractors to conduct a site visit for any Medicare provider or supplier.

[46] A surety bond is a three-party agreement in which a company, known as a surety, agrees to compensate the bondholder if the bond purchaser fails to keep a specified promise.

[47] Social Security Act § 1834(a)(16)(B). [48]PPACA, § 6402, 124 Stat. 119, 753-763.

[49] HHS-OIG, *Use of Surety Bonds to Recover Overpayments Made to Suppliers of Durable Medical Equipment, Prosthetics, Orthotics, and Supplies: Early Findings*, OEI-03-11-00351 (Sept. 12, 2011).

[50] The guidance states that payment from the surety bond includes amounts up to the maximum obligation of the bond including: the amount of any unpaid claim, plus accrued interest, for which the DMEPOS supplier is responsible; and the amount of any unpaid claim, civil monetary penalty, or assessment imposed by CMS or the HHS OIG on the DMEPOS supplier, plus accrued interest.

[51] Channelers are contractors who help collect the criminal history record information for the FBI. FBI-approved channelers receive the fingerprint submission and relevant data, collect the associated fee(s), electronically forward the fingerprint submission with the necessary information to the FBI for a national criminal background check, and receive the electronic record check result for dissemination to the individual or authorized recipient.

In: Fraud Detection and Deterrence ... ISBN: 978-1-62417-658-6
Editor: Anton Ferilli

Chapter 7

PROGRAM INTEGRITY: FURTHER ACTION NEEDED TO ADDRESS VULNERABILITIES IN MEDICAID AND MEDICARE PROGRAMS. STATEMENT OF CAROLYN L. YOCOM, DIRECTOR, HEALTH CARE AND KATHLEEN M. KING, DIRECTOR, HEALTH CARE, GOVERNMENT ACCOUNTABILITY OFFICE. HEARING ON "ASSESSING MEDICARE AND MEDICAID PROGRAM INTEGRITY"*

WHY GAO DID THIS STUDY

In 2011, CMS estimated that Medicaid and Medicare had improper payments of $21.9 billion and almost $43 billion, respectively—among the largest for all federal programs. Both health care programs are on GAO's list of high-risk programs. Over the years, Congress has passed legislation designed to help address program integrity issues in the two programs but they remain vulnerable to fraud, waste, and abuse. The program integrity challenges are different for Medicaid and Medicare. With 51 distinct state-

* This is an edited, reformatted and augmented version of a Statement given on June 7, 2012 before the House Committee on Oversight and Government Reform, Subcommittee on Government Organization, Efficiency, and Financial Management.

based programs, Medicaid has complex challenges for finding the appropriate balance between state and federal efforts. Medicare uses contractors to help administer the program and CMS must oversee their efforts. This statement examines the progress made and important steps still to be taken in these programs. GAO focused on four key strategies and recommendations that were designed to facilitate them that were identified in prior work and that could help reduce improper payments: (1) strengthening provider enrollment standards and procedures to ensure that only legitimate providers participate in the program; (2) improving prepayment controls; (3) improving postpayment claims review and recovery of improper payments; and (4) developing a robust process for addressing identified vulnerabilities. This statement is based on GAO products issued from April 2004 through May 2012 and interviews with agency officials and other stakeholders. In May 2012, GAO also received additional information from CMS on agency actions. GAO received technical comments from CMS officials and incorporated them into this statement.

WHAT GAO FOUND

For the Medicaid program, the Centers for Medicare & Medicaid Services (CMS) and the states have taken some actions related to GAO's four key strategies but more needs to be done.

- CMS's comprehensive state program integrity reviews identified provider enrollment as the most frequently cited area of concern but the agency has noted a positive trend in states' awareness of regulatory requirements.
- CMS noted vulnerabilities in the prepayment reviews of claims in five states and effective practices in seven others. In anticipation of new analytic tools to predict vulnerabilities before claims are paid, the agency has initiated discussions with and provided guidance to states.
- CMS has begun collaborating with states to identify targets for federal postpayment audits, which should help to avoid duplication of federal and state audit efforts.
- CMS has not established a robust process for states to evaluate and address vulnerabilities identified by the states' new recovery audit contractors brought in to identify improper payments and recoup overpayments.

For the Medicare program, CMS has acted to strengthen several of its strategies to better ensure program integrity, but other actions remain undone.

- Congress authorized CMS to implement several new or improved enrollment safeguards, including screening enrollment applications for categories of Medicare providers by risk level. CMS has issued a final rule to implement this and other changes, but has not completed other final rules and additional actions that could further strengthen enrollment procedures, such as rules to implement new surety bond provisions and provider and supplier disclosures.
- GAO's prior work found certain gaps in Medicare's prepayment edits based on coverage and payment policies and made recommendations for improvement, such as adding edits to identify abnormally rapid increases in medical equipment billing. GAO is currently evaluating new CMS efforts in this area.
- CMS has begun using recovery auditing in its prescription drug program but not for its Medicare managed care plans.
- GAO recommended that CMS establish an adequate process to ensure prompt resolution of identified vulnerabilities in Medicare and is currently evaluating steps that CMS has taken recently.

It is critical that CMS and the states continue working on reducing improper payments. While both have made efforts to reduce improper payments, further action is needed. Although Medicaid presents different challenges, GAO believes that many of the lessons learned from its work on Medicare could be applied to strengthen Medicaid program integrity. These lessons can be applied as CMS and the states begin to use the additional tools provided through recent legislation. As the implementation process proceeds, GAO is continuing to monitor these issues. Effectively implementing provisions of recent laws and GAO's recommendations will be critical to reducing improper payments and ensuring that federal funds are used efficiently and for their intended purpose.

Chairman Platts, Ranking Member Towns, and Members of the Subcommittee:

We are pleased to be here today to discuss our work regarding program integrity efforts in the Medicaid and Medicare programs. Medicaid and Medicare are two of the largest programs in the federal government, financing health care services for a combined total of approximately 119 million individuals at a cost of about $983 billion in 2011.[1] These two programs also have some of the largest reported estimates of improper payments—payments that either were made in an incorrect amount or should not have been made at all.[2] The Centers for Medicare & Medicaid Services (CMS), the agency within the Department of Health and Human Services (HHS) that oversees Medicaid and Medicare, has estimated that improper payments in the Medicaid program were $21.9 billion in fiscal year 2011.[3] For the Medicare program, CMS estimated improper payments of almost $43 billion in fiscal year 2011.[4] In part because of concerns over improper payments, we have identified both as high-risk programs.[5]

The program integrity challenges are different for Medicaid and Medicare. With 51 distinct state-based programs that are partially federally financed, Medicaid has complex challenges for finding the appropriate balance of state and federal efforts to ensure its integrity.[6] States are the first line of defense against Medicaid improper payments because they are responsible for ensuring the qualifications of providers who bill the program, detecting improper payments, recovering overpayments, and referring suspected cases of fraud and abuse to law enforcement authorities. However, CMS has a critical role ensuring that adequate controls are in place and states' actions to help reduce improper payments are effective—which involves balancing the agency's oversight and support roles. The Medicaid Integrity Group—an organization within CMS's Center for Program Integrity—is responsible for the Medicaid Integrity Program, which focuses on overseeing and supporting state program integrity activities. Medicare's challenges are also significant. Since its inception, Medicare has been administered largely by contractors with federal oversight. 7 In Medicare Parts A and B, CMS contractors process and pay approximately 4.5 million claims per workday, manage the information technology payment systems, enroll providers, respond to beneficiary questions, and investigate potential Medicare fraud. In Medicare Advantage (Part C) and the Medicare prescription drug benefit (Part D), CMS contracts with private health plans and drug sponsors to administer the Medicare benefits. In that capacity, the plans and sponsors have a responsibility to help ensure Medicare program integrity, and CMS must oversee their efforts to help ensure proper payments. The Medicare Integrity Group, also located within CMS's Center for Program Integrity, is responsible for the Medicare Integrity Program. However, other CMS components, such as the Office of Financial Management and the Center for Medicare, also share significant responsibilities for overseeing activities to ensure the integrity of the program.

Our testimony today focuses on the progress CMS has made and important steps still to be taken to better assure the integrity of the Medicaid and Medicare programs. We will focus on four key strategies and recommendations designed to facilitate them that were identified in our prior work and that can help reduce improper payments:

- Strengthening provider enrollment standards and procedures to help reduce the risk of enrolling entities intent on defrauding the program;
- Improving prepayment controls, to ensure that claims are paid correctly the first time;
- Improving postpayment claims review and recovery of improper payments to reduce the likelihood of and recoup overpayments; and
- Developing a robust process for tackling identified vulnerabilities in order to address risks that lead to improper payments.

This testimony is largely based on products that were issued from April 2004 through May 2012.[8] In addition, to assess CMS and state efforts to strengthen provider enrollment standards and procedures and improve prepayment and postpayment claims review for Medicaid, we analyzed CMS's comprehensive reviews of state program integrity activities and its audits of state Medicaid providers. This additional work was performed in May 2012. We also received updated information from CMS in May 2012 on its actions related to the laws, regulations, guidance, and open recommendations that we discuss in this statement. We shared the facts contained in this statement with CMS and have incorporated their comments as appropriate. Our work was conducted in accordance with generally accepted government auditing standards. Those standards require that we plan and perform the audit to obtain sufficient, appropriate evidence to provide a reasonable basis for our findings and conclusions based on our audit objectives. We believe that the evidence obtained provides a reasonable basis for our findings and conclusions based on our audit objectives.

BACKGROUND

Since 1996, Congress has taken important steps to increase program integrity funding and oversight, including the establishment of both the Medicaid and Medicare Integrity Programs. Table 1 summarizes several key congressional actions.

Table 1. Key Congressional Actions to Increase Program Integrity Funding and Oversight in the Medicaid and Medicare Programs

Year	Congressional action	Statute
1996	Created the Medicare Integrity Program and established a dedicated fund for activities to address fraud, waste, and abuse in federal health care programs, including both Medicaid and Medicare[a]	Health Insurance Portability and Accountability Act of 1996[b]
2003	Directed CMS to conduct a 3-year demonstration project on the use of a new type of contractors—recovery audit contractors (RAC)—in identifying underpayments and overpayments, and recouping Medicare overpayments	Medicare Prescription Drug, Improvement, and Modernization Act of 2003[c]
2006	Established the Medicaid Integrity Program to support and oversee state Medicaid program integrity activities and included specific appropriations to reduce fraud, waste, and abuse	Deficit Reduction Act of 2005[d]
2010	Provided additional funding for program integrity activities and, among other things: • Required states to establish Medicaid RACs and CMS to extend the Medicare RACs to Parts C and D of the Medicare program • Established new provider enrollment requirements for both programs • Required CMS to develop core elements for provider compliance programs • Authorized surety bond requirements for providers[e]	Patient Protection and Affordable Care Act[f]
2010	Required Medicare to begin using predictive analytics to identify and prevent fraud, with their use in Medicaid by 2015 to be based on the results of Medicare's experience[g]	Small Business Jobs Act of 2010[h]

Source: GAO analysis of selected federal laws.

[a] The fund is known as the Health Care Fraud and Abuse Control account.

[b] Pub. L. No. 104-191, §§ 201-202, 110 Stat. 1936, 1993, 1996 (codified at 42 U.S. C. §§ 1395i, 1395ddd).

[c] Pub. L. No. 108-173, § 306, 117 Stat. 2066, 2256-57. Subsequently, the Tax Relief and Health Care Act of 2006 required CMS to implement a national recovery audit contractor program by January 1, 2010. Pub. L. No. 109-432, div B., title III, § 302, 120 Stat. 2922, 2991-92 (codified at 42 U.S.C. § 1395 ddd(h)).

[d] See Pub. L. No. 109-171, § 6034, 120 Stat. 4, 74-78 (2006) (codified at 42 U.S.C. § 1396u-6).

[e] A surety bond is a three-party agreement in which a company, known as a surety, agrees to compensate the bondholder if the bond purchaser fails to keep a specified promise.

[f] Pub. L. No. 111-148, 124 Stat. 119 (2010), as amended by the Health Care Education Reconciliation Act of 2010, Pub. L. No. 111-152, 124 Stat. 1029.

[g] Predictive analytics include the use of algorithms and models to analyze claims before payment is made in order to identify unusual or suspicious patterns or abnormalities in provider networks, claims billing patterns, and beneficiary utilization.

[h] Pub. L. No. 111-240, § 4241, 124 Stat. 2504, 2599.

CMS AND STATES HAVE UNDERTAKEN EFFORTS TO IMPROVE MEDICAID PROGRAM INTEGRITY, BUT MORE NEEDS TO BE DONE

CMS and the states are continuing to strengthen provider enrollment standards and procedures, as well as developing adequate controls to detect improper claims before they are paid. While CMS has made progress in collaborating more closely with states on federal postpayment claims reviews by shifting the focus to state-identified targets, it is too early to assess the potential for Medicaid recovery audit contractors (RAC) to avoid duplicating efforts of ongoing state and federal provider audits. Finally, the agency has not established a robust process for incorporating RAC-identified vulnerabilities in state corrective action plans.

Provider Enrollment Standards Remain a Concern, but CMS Has Reported Some Progress

CMS and the states continue efforts to strengthen the standards and procedures for enrolling Medicaid providers, which could help reduce the risk of enrolling providers intent on defrauding or abusing the program. Since 2007, CMS has monitored states' Medicaid provider enrollment standards and procedures—as well as other aspects of their programs— through comprehensive state program integrity reviews.[9] The Patient Protection and Affordable Care Act (PPACA) also included several provisions aimed at strengthening Medicaid provider enrollment standards and procedures.[10] For example, PPACA required states to conduct certain provider screening procedures, such as verifying provider licenses and terminating individuals or entities from Medicaid participation under certain circumstances.[11]

Our analysis of final reports from CMS's most recent comprehensive reviews for all 51 states found 230 instances of non-compliance with federal laws or federal regulatory requirements related to states' provider enrollment standards and procedures.[12] Most of the reviews we analyzed were conducted prior to CMS's final rule implementing PPACA provider enrollment provisions.[13] CMS cited at least 1 instance and as many as 8 instances of non-compliance for each state reviewed, with 31 states receiving 4 or 5 citations. About half of the citations were generally due to states' failures to verify provider licenses, or collect or disclose required ownership and related information.[14] In the introduction to its summary of 2011 comprehensive reviews, CMS noted that provider enrollment has been the most frequently cited area of non-compliance since it began these reviews in 2007. While these problems were identified in nearly every state, CMS also reported that it had noticed a positive trend in states' awareness of regulatory requirements and knowledge of how to implement the requirements.

In addition to identifying areas in which states needed to improve their provider enrollment standards and procedures, CMS's most recent comprehensive reviews of all 51 states identified a total of 53 instances of effective or noteworthy provider enrollment practices.[15] CMS credited 29 states with having at least one effective or noteworthy practice, and deemed 1 state to have five. For example, CMS found that this state had

- an innovative software package that automated the verification of licenses of potential Medicaid providers, which ensures that Medicaid does not allow payments to nonqualified health care providers;
- a team dedicated to conducting criminal background checks prior to approving a provider application; and
- a requirement that managed care providers be enrolled in Medicaid before they are eligible to become a member of a participating managed care plan's provider network, which ensures that such providers will have had a criminal background check conducted by the state.

In addition to the comprehensive reviews, CMS provided guidance periodically to states. In August 2010, CMS issued guidance to states on best practices related to provider enrollment. Among other things, this guidance recommended that states meet regularly and coordinate enrollment policy with provider enrollment personnel, ensure that provider enrollment forms request all required disclosures, and report to the HHS Office of Inspector General (OIG) any adverse actions taken on providers' Medicaid participation and providers' criminal convictions. In July 2011, the Medicaid Integrity Institute—CMS's national Medicaid training program for state program integrity officials—sponsored a symposium on PPACA's program integrity enhancements—including the provider enrollment provisions—and discussed strategies to achieve their timely implementation.

CMS Continues to Monitor States' Implementation and Use of Prepayment Claims Review

While states are responsible for paying claims and conducting prepayment reviews of claims, CMS is responsible for ensuring that states have adequate controls to detect improper claims before they are paid. Two ways CMS provides this oversight are through (1) an examination of states' prepayment review processes, which occurs during CMS's comprehensive state program integrity reviews, and (2) the provision of guidance to states on their use of predictive analytics, which use algorithms and models to simultaneously analyze large numbers of claims from multiple data sources before payment is made in order to identify unusual or suspicious patterns or abnormalities in provider networks, claims billing patterns, and beneficiary utilization.

Although not all of CMS's comprehensive reviews included information on states' prepayment review processes, our analysis of the most recent comprehensive reviews for all 51 states noted vulnerabilities in the processes of 5 states and regulatory compliance issues in 1 state. For example, CMS found that 1 state did not conduct prepayment reviews or suspend or withhold payments to providers suspected of fraud and abuse. Rather, the state only withheld provider payments after determining that it had overpaid a provider. For another state, a very limited prepayment review process was seen as one of many issues contributing to what CMS characterized as the state's ineffective program integrity oversight and operations.

These comprehensive reviews also noted effective and noteworthy prepayment review processes in 7 states. For example, CMS highlighted one state's prepayment edit process that included an automated edit system to deny claims that failed to meet certain standards.[16] For another state, CMS recognized the state's efforts to effectively communicate program integrity concerns throughout its Medicaid agency; these communications included the establishment of an agencywide committee—with representation from the program integrity division—that regularly discussed current and proposed edits for inclusion in prepayment reviews.

According to CMS officials, they have had discussions with and provided guidance and technical assistance to states regarding the use of predictive analytics to identify and prevent improper payments both informally and during three recent Medicaid Integrity Institute symposiums. CMS officials also told us that states are in varying stages of implementing predictive analytics; based on Medicare's experience, the Small Business Jobs Act of 2010 requires the use of predictive analytics in Medicaid beginning in 2015.[17]

Federal Postpayment Claims Reviews Are Becoming More Collaborative; Introduction of Recovery Audit Contractors Will Need to Avoid Duplication with Other Audit Efforts

Our prior work found that postpayment reviews are critical to identifying and recouping overpayments, but the importance of collaboration and coordination to avoid duplication has grown because of the increase in the number of entities other than states now conducting such reviews.18,19 In 2011, we reported that collaborative audits were a promising approach to avoiding duplication of federal and state audit efforts.[20]

As directed by the Deficit Reduction Act of 2005, CMS established a federal program to audit state Medicaid claims. Since implementing federal audits in 2008, CMS's contractors have conducted a total of 1,662 postpayment audits, 1,550 of which were federal audits where CMS identified the audit targets and 112 of which were collaborative audits where CMS relied on state Medicaid integrity programs to identify audit targets.[21] Our analysis shows that since shifting to a more collaborative approach in 2010, the focus of audits has changed from an emphasis on hospitals to an emphasis on long-term care and pharmacy (see table 2).

Table 2. Number and Percentage of Provider Types Targeted by Federal and Collaborative Audits

Provider type	Number of federal audits	Percentage of all federal audits[a]	Number of collaborative audits	Percentage of collaborative audits[a]
Hospital	584	38	11	10
Long-term care	284	18	33	29
Physician	227	15	8	7
Pharmacy	225	15	35	31
Home health	9	1	6	5
Durable medical equipment	45	3	1	1
Other	176	11	18	16
Total	1,550	100	112	100

Source: GAO analysis of CMS data.

Note: Data presented from 2008 through February 29, 2012. "Other" includes clinic, behavioral health, dental, personal care, managed care, hospice, ambulatory health care facilities, direct service providers, disability care services, home office, provider agency, transportation, therapeutic residential child care facility, and cases that CMS labeled "other."

[a]Column does not add up to 100 due to rounding.

PPACA requires state Medicaid programs to establish contracts with RACs, consistent with state law and similar to the contracts established for the Medicare program, subject to exceptions or requirements provided by CMS.[22] One or more of these RACs are to identify and recoup overpayments and identify underpayments made for services provided by state Medicaid programs. The National Association of Medicaid Directors (NAMD) in March 2012 noted concern about the potential for overlap between federal and state program integrity activities, particularly with respect to provider audits, and observed that the deployment of Medicaid RACs increased the potential for duplication.[23] CMS's shift to collaborative federal audits should help resolve the potential for duplication of state audit efforts because states identify the collaborative audit targets. However, a few states that we discussed the Medicaid RAC program with voiced concerns about the potential for duplication with their own audits. In its September 2011 final rule implementing the Medicaid RAC program, CMS disagreed with similar public comments that the Medicaid RAC program would duplicate efforts of the federal national audit program because federal audit targets are vetted with states.[24] In this final rule, CMS acknowledged the potential for the duplication of efforts among different auditing entities and required states to coordinate their RAC efforts with other auditing entities. According to CMS, RACs are an efficient way to identify payment errors, while federal audits may be more effective in identifying or preventing fraudulent practices.

CMS defined implementation of state RAC programs to mean that states must have a signed contract in place with their selected contractors by January 1, 2012. According to agency officials, 32 states had signed contracts with RAC vendors as of May 31, 2012, but few states' Medicaid RAC programs were operational. In addition, officials told us that 17 states had requested exceptions due to implementation delays. The few states with operational RAC programs had not yet reported on whether RACs had increased state collections of improper payments. As a result, it is too early to assess the initial results and the potential for duplication, including the steps CMS and the states will take to avoid duplication.

CMS Has Not Established a Robust Process for Incorporating Identified Vulnerabilities in State Corrective Action Plans

Our prior work has demonstrated that CMS had not developed a robust process to specifically address identified vulnerabilities that lead to improper payments in Medicaid. Previously we reported that CMS, in its proposed rule for the Medicaid RAC program, did not include steps for states to collect information on RAC-identified vulnerabilities and to develop a corrective action plan to address them.[25] CMS requires state Medicaid agencies to have a corrective action process as part of their activities to reduce their Medicaid error rates. Information from the Medicaid RAC program could be incorporated into these processes. In response to a comment on the proposed rule noting this weakness, CMS acknowledged the importance of having RAC-identified vulnerabilities incorporated in state program integrity activities, observing, "if Medicaid RACs identify program vulnerabilities as a result of their findings, we encourage RACs to share this information with States so that they can implement corrective action, such as pre-payment edits or other similar system fixes."[26] However, CMS did not incorporate a process for states to evaluate and address RAC-identified vulnerabilities into its final rule.

CMS Has Made Progress in Strengthening Its Medicare Program Integrity Efforts, but Further Actions Are Needed

CMS has made progress strengthening several of the strategies to better ensure the integrity of the Medicare program, such as implementing changes to provider enrollment. However, CMS has not completed other actions that could be helpful in addressing improper payments and reducing fraud, waste and abuse in the Medicare program, including implementation of some relevant PPACA provisions and some of our prior recommendations.

CMS Has Taken Action on Certain PPACA Provider Enrollment Provisions, but Not Completed Others

To address past weaknesses that allowed entities intent on committing fraud from enrolling in Medicare, PPACA authorized CMS to implement several actions to strengthen provider enrollment, some of which have been completed. Specifically, CMS has added screenings of categories of provider enrollment applications by risk level and new national enrollment screening and site visit contractors.

Screening Provider Enrollment Applications by Risk Level: CMS and the HHS-OIG issued a final rule with comment period in February 2011 to implement many of the new screening procedures required by PPACA.[27] CMS designated three levels of risk—high, moderate, and limited—with different screening procedures for categories of Medicare providers at each level. Providers in the high-risk level are subject to the most rigorous screening.[28] Based in part on our work and that of the HHS-OIG, CMS designated newly enrolling home health agencies and durable medical equipment, prosthetics, orthotics, and supplies (DMEPOS) suppliers as high risk and designated other providers at lower levels. Providers at all risk levels are screened to verify that they meet specific requirements established by Medicare, such as having current licenses or accreditation and valid Social Security numbers.[29] High- and moderate-risk providers are additionally subject to unannounced site visits. Further, depending on the risks presented, PPACA authorizes CMS to require fingerprint-based criminal history checks, and the posting of surety bonds for certain providers.[30]

CMS indicated in the discussion of the final rule that the agency will continue to review the criteria for its screening levels on an ongoing basis and would publish changes if the agency decided to update the assignment of screening levels for categories of Medicare providers. Doing so could become important because the Department of Justice (DOJ) and HHS reported multiple convictions or other legal actions against types of providers not currently at the high-risk level, including medical clinics and physical therapy practices.[31] CMS's implementation of accreditation for DMEPOS suppliers, and of a competitive bidding program, including in areas thought to have high fraud rates, may be helping to reduce risk of DMEPOS fraud.[32] As a result, while continued vigilance on DMEPOS suppliers is warranted, other types of providers may become more problematic in the future. We are currently examining the types of providers involved in fraud cases investigated by the HHSOIG and DOJ, which may help illuminate risk to the Medicare program from different types of providers.

New National Enrollment Screening and Site Visit Contractors: CMS contracted with two new types of entities at the end of 2011 to assume centralized responsibility for two functions that had been the responsibility of multiple contractors. One of the new contractors will be conducting automated screening to check that providers and suppliers have valid licensure, accreditation, a valid National Provider Identifier (NPI), and no presence on the HHS-OIG list of providers and suppliers excluded from participating in federal health care programs. The second contractor has begun conducting site visits of providers to determine if sites are legitimate and the providers meet certain Medicare standards.[33] CMS officials told us that the agency expects that these new contractors will provide more efficiency and consistency in their reviews.

However, our prior work found that CMS had not implemented other enrollment screening actions authorized by PPACA. These actions could help further reduce the enrollment of providers and suppliers intent on defrauding the Medicare program. They include issuing a rule to implement surety bonds for providers, completing contract awards to begin fingerprint-based criminal background checks, issuing a rule on provider and supplier disclosure requirements, and establishing the core elements for provider and supplier compliance programs.

Surety Bond: PPACA authorizes CMS to require a surety bond for certain types of at-risk providers. Surety bonds may serve as a source for recoupment of erroneous payments. CMS has not developed a proposed rule to require surety bonds as conditions of enrollment to implement this requirement. Extending the use of surety bonds to these new entities would augment a previous statutory requirement for DMEPOS suppliers to post a surety bond at the time of enrollment.[34] While CMS had required surety bonds from DMEPOS suppliers since 2009, CMS did not issue instructions for recovering overpayments through surety bonds, until January 2012, to take effect in February 2012. As of May 2012, CMS had not collected any funds from surety bond companies.

Fingerprint-based Criminal Background Checks: CMS officials told us that they are working with the Federal Bureau of Investigation to arrange a contract that will enable the agency to access information to help conduct fingerprint-based criminal background checks of high-risk providers and suppliers, which is a tool authorized by PPACA. The agency expects to have the necessary contract in place by early 2013.

Providers and Suppliers Disclosure: CMS had not completed development of regulations for increased disclosures of prior actions taken against providers and suppliers enrolling or revalidating enrollment in Medicare, such as whether the provider or supplier has been subject to a payment suspension from a federal health care program.[35] Agency officials indicated that developing the additional disclosure requirements was complicated by provider and supplier concerns about what types of information will be collected, what CMS will do with it, and how the privacy and security of this information will be maintained.

Compliance Program: CMS had not established the core elements of compliance programs for providers and suppliers, as required by PPACA. Agency officials indicated that they had sought public comments on the core elements, which they were considering, and were also studying criteria found in HHS-OIG model plans for possible inclusion.[36]

Additional Improvements to Prepayment Claims Review May Better Identify Improper Payments

Increased efforts to review claims on a prepayment basis can better prevent payments that should not be made. As claims go through Medicare's electronic claims payment systems, they are subjected to prepayment edits, most of which are fully automated; if a claim does not meet the criteria of the edit, it is automatically denied. Other prepayment edits are manual; they flag a claim for individual review by trained staff who determine if it should be paid. Due to the volume of claims, CMS has reported that less than 1 percent of Medicare claims are subject to manual medical record review by trained personnel.

Having effective prepayment edits that deny claims for ineligible providers and suppliers depends on having timely and accurate information about them, such as whether the providers are currently enrolled and have the appropriate license or accreditation to provide specific services. We have previously identified flaws in the timeliness and accuracy of data in the Provider Enrollment Chain and Ownership System (PECOS)—the database that maintains Medicare provider and supplier enrollment information, which may result in CMS making improper payments to ineligible providers and suppliers.[37] These weaknesses are related to the frequency with which CMS's contractors update enrollment information and the timeliness and accuracy of information obtained from outside entities, such as state licensing boards,[38] the HHS-OIG, and the Social Security Administration's Death Master File, which contains information on deceased individuals that can be used to identify deceased providers in order to deactivate their NPI. CMS has indicated that its new national screening contractor should improve the timeliness and accuracy of the provider and supplier information in PECOS by centralizing the process, increasing automation of the process, checking databases more frequently, and incorporating new sources of data, such as financial, business, tax, and geospatial data. We are planning to review the accuracy of PECOS information.

Having effective edits to implement coverage and payment policies before payment is made can also prevent improper payments. The Medicare program has defined categories of items and services eligible for coverage and excludes from coverage items or services that are determined not to be "reasonable and necessary for the diagnosis and treatment of an illness or injury or to improve functioning of a malformed body part." [39] CMS and its contractors set policies regarding when and how items and services will be covered by Medicare, as well as coding and billing requirements for payment, which can be implemented in the payment systems through edits. Our prior work found certain gaps in Medicare's prepayment edits based on coverage and payment policies and made recommendations for improvement, which have not all been implemented. For example, CMS has not developed edits to identify abnormally rapid increases in billing by DMEPOS suppliers, which is associated with fraudulent billing.[40] We are currently assessing CMS's implementation of edits on coverage and payment policies.

We are also currently evaluating a new CMS effort, the Fraud Prevention System (FPS), which uses predictive analytic technologies to analyze Medicare fee-for-service (FFS) claims as required by the Small Business Jobs Act of 2010. According to CMS, FPS may enhance CMS's ability to identify potential fraud because it simultaneously analyzes large numbers of claims from multiple data sources nationwide before payment is made, thus allowing CMS to examine billing patterns across geographic regions for those that may indicate fraud. The results of FPS could lead to the initiation of payment suspensions, implementation of automatic claim denials, and identification of additional prepayment edits, investigations, or the revocation of Medicare billing privileges. CMS began using FPS to screen all FFS claims nationwide prior to payment as of June 30, 2011. Because FPS is relatively new, and we have not completed our work, it is too soon to determine whether FPS will improve CMS's ability to address fraud.

Adding New Contractors and Taking Additional Actions Could Improve Medicare Postpayment Claims Reviews

Adding new RACs into the Medicare program may help in identifying under or overpayments, and in recouping overpayments.[41] Prior to PPACA, CMS began a national RAC program in March 2009 for FFS Medicare.[42] As of May 2012, CMS reported that $1.86 billion was recouped due to these contractors' efforts from October 2009 through March 2012.

PPACA required the expansion of Medicare RACs to Parts C and D. CMS has implemented a RAC for Part D, but not for Part C.

- The agency awarded a Part D RAC task order[43] for a 1-year base period that began in January 2011, and 4 option years. The Part D RAC is modeled after the Medicare FFS RACs and conducts postpayment review of Part D claims for prescription drugs based on specific criteria determined by CMS. CMS has approved the Part D RAC to conduct postpayment review of claims to identify several issues leading to improper payments, such as payments to excluded providers and duplicate payments.[44] To ensure that the Part D RAC is making correct determinations of any improper payments, CMS has included a validation contractor to review Part D RAC determinations. CMS officials stated that the Part D RAC has started its review of 2007 claims data for prescription drug events and has identified potential overpayments to recoup.
- CMS has not yet awarded a Part C RAC task order or contract. Agency officials indicated that they are still considering different options for implementing a Part C RAC program to address improper Medicare Advantage plan payments. Plans are paid a monthly capitated per-person payment for enrolled beneficiaries, based on an approved bid amount and risk adjusted based on individual beneficiaries' health status. Most of the Part C payment errors are driven by errors in the risk adjustment data (clinical diagnosis data) submitted by the plans, due to diagnoses not supported by the medical records. CMS is currently auditing Part C plans' reporting of risk adjustment data. CMS officials indicated concern that adding additional contractors to identify Medicare Advantage plan payment errors would duplicate current efforts.

Further actions are also needed to improve use of two CMS information technology systems that could help analysts identify fraud after claims have been paid.[45]

- The Integrated Data Repository (IDR) became operational in September 2006 as a central data store of Medicare and other data needed to help CMS program integrity staff and contractors detect improper payments of claims. However, we found IDR did not include all the data that were planned to be incorporated by fiscal year

2010, because of technical obstacles and delays in funding. Further, as of December 2011, the agency had not finalized plans or developed reliable schedules for efforts to incorporate these data, which could lead to additional delays.

- One Program Integrity (One PI) is a web-based portal intended to provide CMS staff and contractors with a single source of access to data contained in IDR, as well as tools for analyzing those data. Although One PI is operational, as of May 2011, CMS had trained few program integrity analysts and the system was not being widely used.

GAO recommended that CMS take steps to finalize plans and reliable schedules for fully implementing and expanding the use of both IDR and One PI and to define measurable benefits. The agency has initiated activities to incorporate additional data into IDR and expand the use of One PI through additional user training. For example, CMS officials indicated that they began incorporating additional Medicare claims data into IDR in September 2011 and as of November 2011, had trained over 200 analysts who were using One PI. CMS officials reported having provided additional training in 2012. However, as of April 2012, CMS had not fully addressed our recommendations—for example, the agency had not finalized plans for adding Medicaid data into IDR.

Robust Process to Address Identified Vulnerabilities Could Help Reduce Improper Payments

Having mechanisms in place to resolve vulnerabilities that lead to improper payments is critical to effective program management, but our work has shown weaknesses in CMS's processes to address such vulnerabilities.[46] Our March 2010 report on the RAC demonstration program found that CMS had not established an adequate process during the demonstration or in planning for the national program to ensure prompt resolution of identified vulnerabilities in Medicare. Further, most vulnerabilities identified during the demonstration were not addressed.[47] We therefore recommended that CMS develop and implement a corrective action process that includes policies and procedures to ensure the agency promptly (1) evaluates findings of RAC audits, (2) decides on the appropriate response and a time frame for taking action based on established criteria, and (3) acts to correct the vulnerabilities identified.[48] In December 2011, the HHS-OIG found that CMS had not resolved or taken significant action to resolve 48 of 62 vulnerabilities reported in 2009 by CMS contractors specifically charged with addressing fraud.[49] The HHS-OIG made several recommendations, including that CMS have written procedures and time frames to assure that vulnerabilities were resolved. CMS has indicated that it is now tracking vulnerabilities identified from several types of contractors through a single vulnerability tracking process, and the agency has developed some written guidance on the process. We are currently examining aspects of CMS's vulnerability tracking process and will be reporting on it soon.

CONCLUSION

CMS and the states must continue and improve their efforts to reduce improper payments. Identifying the nature, extent, and underlying causes of improper payments, and developing adequate corrective action processes to address vulnerabilities, is an essential prerequisite to reducing them. Although Medicaid presents different challenges, we believe that many of the lessons learned from our Medicare work could be applied to strengthen Medicaid program integrity. These lessons can be applied as CMS and the states begin to use the additional tools to identify and recoup Medicaid improper payments provided through recent legislation. As CMS and the states implement these PPACA and Small Business Jobs Act provisions, additional evaluation and oversight will help determine whether the provisions are implemented as intended and have the desired effect on better ensuring proper payments. Moreover, we are continuing to monitor CMS and state efforts as the implementation process proceeds. Notably, we have work under way assessing CMS's efforts to support and strengthen Medicaid program integrity through its Medicaid Integrity Program. We are also examining the effectiveness of different types of prepayment edits in Medicare, including CMS's oversight of its contractors in implementing those edits, and CMS's implementation of predictive analytics through FPS. The level of importance placed on effectively implementing our recommendations and the provisions of recent laws will be critical to reducing improper payments in the Medicaid and Medicare programs, and ensuring that federal funds are used efficiently and for their intended purposes.

Chairman Platts, Ranking Member Towns, and Members of the Subcommittee, this completes our prepared statement. We would be pleased to respond to any questions that you may have at this time.

APPENDIX I: ABBREVIATIONS

CMS	Centers for Medicare & Medicaid Services
DOJ	Department of Justice
DMEPOS	durable medical equipment, prosthetics, orthotics and supplies
FFS	fee-for-service
FPS	Fraud Prevention System
HHS	Department of Health and Human Services
IDR	Integrated Data Repository
NAMD	National Association of Medicaid Directors
NPI	National Provider Identifier
OIG	Office of Inspector General
PECOS	Provider Enrollment Chain and Ownership System
PPACA	Patient Protection and Affordable Care Act
RAC	recovery audit contractor

End Notes

[1] Medicaid is the federal-state program that covers acute health care, long-term care, and other services for certain low-income people. It is also one of the largest components of state budgets. In 2011, Medicaid covered approximately 70 million people and estimated expenditures totaled about $427 billion, with a federal share of $271 billion and a state share of $157 billion (numbers do not add due to rounding). Medicare is the federally financed health insurance program for persons age 65 or over, certain individuals with disabilities, and individuals with end-stage renal disease. In 2011, Medicare covered almost 49 million people at an estimated cost of about $556 billion.

[2] An improper payment is any payment that should not have been made or that was made in an incorrect amount (including overpayments and underpayments) under statutory, contractual, administrative, or other legally applicable requirements. This definition includes any payment to an ineligible recipient, any payment for an ineligible good or service, any duplicate payment, any payment for a good or service not received (except where authorized by law), and any payment that does not account for credit for applicable discounts. Improper Payments Elimination and Recovery Act of 2010, Pub. L. No. 111-204, § 2(e), 124 Stat. 2224, 2227 (codified at 31 U.S.C. § 3321 note). Improper payments may be a result of fraud, waste, and abuse. Fraud represents intentional acts or

representations to deceive with knowledge that the action or representation could result in an inappropriate gain. Waste includes inaccurate payments for services, such as unintentional duplicate payments. Abuse represents actions inconsistent with acceptable business or medical practices.

[3] In its *Fiscal Year 2011 Agency Financial Report*, HHS calculated and reported the 3-year (2009, 2010, and 2011) weighted average national payment error rate for Medicaid of 8.1 percent. See HHS, *Department of Health and Human Services FY 2011 Agency Financial Report* (Washington, D.C.: Nov. 15, 2011).

[4] HHS, *Department of Health and Human Services FY 2011 Agency Financial Report.*

[5] See GAO, *High-Risk Series: An Update*, GAO-11-278 (Washington, D.C.: February 2011).

[6] While American Samoa, Guam, the Commonwealth of the Northern Mariana Islands, the United States Virgin Islands, and Puerto Rico also receive federal funds for Medicaid, this statement focuses on the 50 states and the District of Columbia, which we refer to as 51 states.

[7] The Medicare program consists of four parts: A, B, C, and D. Medicare Parts A and B are known as Medicare fee-for-service (FFS). Medicare Part A covers hospital and other inpatient stays. Medicare Part B is optional, and covers hospital outpatient, physician, and other services. Medicare beneficiaries have the option of obtaining coverage for Medicare services from private health plans that participate in Medicare Advantage—Medicare's managed care program—also known as Part C. All Medicare beneficiaries may purchase coverage for outpatient prescription drugs under Part D, either as a stand-alone benefit or as part of a Medicare Advantage plan.

[8] The products listed at the end of this statement contain detailed information on the methodologies used in our work.

[9] CMS typically conducts triennial comprehensive state program integrity reviews of 16 to 17 states each year. These reviews assess the effectiveness of each state's Medicaid program integrity activities and compliance with federal statutes and regulations. The culmination of a review is a final report that details CMS's assessment of the state's program integrity effective and noteworthy practices, vulnerabilities, and compliance issues.

[10] For purposes of this chapter, we use the term provider to include both providers and suppliers.

[11] Circumstances that warrant termination include if the individual or entity owns, controls, or manages an entity that has unpaid overpayments or is affiliated with an individual or entity that has been suspended, excluded, or terminated from any state's Medicaid program. CMS and the HHS's Office of Inspector General (HHS-OIG) published a final rule regarding provider and supplier screening and enrollment on February 2, 2011, which became effective on March 25, 2011. *Medicare, Medicaid, and Children's Health Insurance Programs; Additional Screening Requirements, Application Fees, Temporary Enrollment Moratoria, Payment Suspensions and Compliance Plans for Providers and Suppliers*, 76 *Fed. Reg.* 5862 (Feb. 2, 2011). CMS also issued additional guidance to states in December 2011.

[12] For our analysis, we included reports from the most recent comprehensive review for each of the 51 states that were available on CMS's website as of May 22, 2012—this included 5 states that were reviewed in 2011, 17 states that were reviewed in 2010, 18 states that were reviewed in 2009, and 11 states that were reviewed in 2008.

[13] CMS officials told us that none of the 16 states that were reviewed during fiscal year 2011 had fully implemented these PPACA provisions. Our analysis only included the fiscal year 2011 report for 5 states that were available on CMS's website as of May 22, 2012; for the other

11 states reviewed during that fiscal year but whose reports were not available online at the time of our analysis, we included the reports from their prior reviews.

[14] In these reviews, CMS also identified areas of vulnerability—areas where changes in states' provider enrollment standards and procedures could potentially reduce the risk of fraud, waste, and abuse.

[15] Some of these noteworthy practices are now required under PPACA. For example, CMS noted that 4 of the states reviewed in 2010 were already screening providers prior to enrollment against some or all of the databases required by PPACA.

[16] CMS's comprehensive reviews focus on states' prepayment review processes, not on the actual edits that states have in place.

[17] Pub. L. No. 111-240, § 4241(c)(3), 124 Stat. 2504, 2600.

[18] See GAO, *Medicare Fraud, Waste, and Abuse: Challenges and Strategies for Preventing Improper Payments,* GAO-10-844T (Washington, D.C.: June 15, 2010).

[19] The Deficit Reduction Act of 2005 required CMS to conduct postpayment audits of state Medicaid claims payments and in 2010 PPACA required states to use audit contractors to recover overpayments and identify underpayments.

[20] GAO, *Medicaid Program Integrity: Expanded Federal Role Presents Challenges to and Opportunities for Assisting States*, GAO-12-288T (Washington, D.C.: Dec. 7, 2011).

[21] We are currently examining the effectiveness of CMS's audits of Medicaid claims—both the federal audits and CMS's redesign of those audits, which CMS refers to as collaborative audits. Specifically, we are examining (1) the effectiveness of CMS's implementation of the national federal audit program, under which it conducted federal audits and (2) its efforts to redesign the national federal audit program, primarily through implementation of collaborative audits. We plan to issue this report in June 2012.

[22] Pub. L. No. 111-148, §6411(a)(1), 124 Stat. 119,773 (codified at 42 U.S.C. § 1396a(a)(42)(B)).

[23] NAMD, *Rethinking Medicaid Program Integrity: Eliminating Duplication and Investing in Effective, High-value Tools* (Washington, D.C.: March 2012).

[24] Medicaid Program: Recovery Audit Contractors, 76 Fed. Reg. 57,808 (Sept. 16, 2011).

[25] See GAO, *Medicare and Medicaid Fraud, Waste, and Abuse: Effective Implementation of Recent Laws and Agency Actions Could Help Reduce Improper Payments,* GAO-11-409T (Washington, D.C.: Mar. 9, 2011). We noted that having Medicaid RACs report to state Medicaid agencies and CMS on the vulnerabilities they identify and having a corrective action process to address those vulnerabilities would be important to reduce Medicaid improper payments.

[26] 76 Fed. Reg. 57808, 57,819.

[27] 76 Fed. Reg. 5862 (Feb. 2, 2011). In discussing the final rule, CMS noted that Medicare had already employed a number of the screening practices described in PPACA to determine if a provider is in compliance with federal and state requirements to enroll or to maintain enrollment in the Medicare program.

[28] PPACA specified that the enhanced screening procedures will apply to new providers and suppliers beginning 1 year after the date of enactment and to currently enrolled providers and suppliers 2 years after that date.

[29] Screening may include verification of the following: Social Security number; National Provider Identifier (NPI); National Practitioner Databank licensure; whether the provider has been excluded from federal health care programs by the HHS-OIG; taxpayer identification number; and death of an individual practitioner, owner, authorized official, delegated official, or supervising physician.

[30] A surety bond is a three-party agreement in which a company, known as a surety, agrees to compensate the bondholder if the bond purchaser fails to keep a specified promise.

[31] *The Department of Health and Human Services and the Department of Justice Health Care Fraud and Abuse Control Program Annual Report for Fiscal Year 2011* (Washington, D.C.: February 2012).

[32] Competitive bidding is a process in which suppliers of medical equipment and supplies compete for the right to provide their products on the basis of established criteria, such as quality and price. See GAO, *Medicare: Review of the First Year of CMS's Durable Medical Equipment Competitive Bidding Program's Round 1 Rebid*, GAO-12-693 (Washington, D.C.: May 9, 2012).

[33] Site visits for DMEPOS suppliers will continue to be conducted by the contractor responsible for their enrollment. In addition, CMS at times exercises its authority to conduct a site visit or request its contractors to conduct a site visit for any Medicare provider or supplier.

[34] 42 U.S.C. § 1395m (a)(16)(B). As of October 2009, DMEPOS suppliers were required to obtain and submit a surety bond in the amount of at least $50,000. A DMEPOS surety bond is a bond issued by an entity guaranteeing that a DMEPOS supplier will fulfill its obligation to Medicare. If the obligation is not met, the surety bond is paid to Medicare. *Medicare Program; Surety Bond Requirement for Suppliers of Durable Medical Equipment, Prosthetics, Orthotics, and Supplies (DMEPOS),* 74 Fed. Reg. 166 (Jan. 2, 2009).

[35] At the time of initial enrollment or revalidation of enrollment, PPACA requires providers and suppliers to disclose any current or previous affiliation with another provider or supplier that has uncollected debt; has been or is subject to a payment suspension under a federal health care program; has been excluded from participation under Medicare, Medicaid, or State Children's Health Insurance Program; or has had its billing privileges denied or revoked.

[36] A compliance program is an internal set of policies, processes, and procedures that a provider organization implements to help it act ethically and lawfully. In this context, a compliance program is intended to help provider and supplier organizations prevent and detect violations of Medicare laws and regulations. The HHS-OIG has developed a series of voluntary compliance program guidance documents directed at various segments of the health care industry, such as hospitals, nursing homes, third-party billers, and durable medical equipment suppliers, to encourage the development and use of internal controls to monitor adherence to applicable statutes, regulations, and program requirements.

[37] See *Medicare Program Integrity: CMS Continues Efforts to Strengthen the Screening of Providers and Suppliers,* GAO-12-351 (Washington, D.C.: Apr. 10, 2012).

[38] Licensure is a mandatory process by which a state government grants permission to an individual practitioner or health care organization to engage in an occupation or profession.

[39] 42 U.S.C. § 1395y(a)(1)(A).

[40] GAO, *Medicare: Improvements Needed to Address Improper Payments for Medical Equipment and Supplies,* GAO-07-59 (Washington, D.C.: Jan. 31, 2007), *Follow-up on 2011 Report: Status of Actions Taken to Reduce Duplication, Overlap, and Fragmentation, Save Tax Dollars, and Enhance Revenue*, GAO-12-453SP (Washington, D.C.: Feb. 28, 2012).

[41] Recovery auditing has been used in various industries, including health care, to identify and collect overpayments for about 40 years.

[42] The Medicare Prescription Drug, Improvement and Modernization Act of 2003 directed CMS to conduct a demonstration of the use of RACs in identifying underpayments and overpayments, and recouping overpayments in Medicare. Pub. L. No. 108-173, § 306, 117 Stat. 2066, 2256-57. Subsequently, in December 2006 the Tax Relief and Health Care Act

of 2006 required CMS to implement a national RAC program by January 1, 2010. Pub. L. No. 109-432, div. B, title III, § 302, 120 Stat. 2924, 2991 (codified at 42 U.S.C. § 1395ddd(h)).

[43] A task order is a supplementary document that outlines specific expected services, supplies, or tasks to be provided under an established contract.

[44] The Part D RAC can propose other issues to audit, but any issue requires prior CMS approval before implementation. CMS limits the number of new audit issues the Part D RAC can propose to a maximum of five a year.

[45] GAO, *Fraud Detection Systems: Centers for Medicare and Medicaid Services Needs to Ensure More Widespread Use*, GAO-11-475 (Washington, D.C.: June 30, 2011).

[46] We have reported that an agency should have policies and procedures to ensure that (1) the findings of all audits and reviews are promptly evaluated, (2) decisions are made about the appropriate response to these findings, and (3) actions are taken to correct or resolve the issues promptly. These are all aspects of internal control, which is the component of an organization's management that provides reasonable assurance that the organization achieves effective and efficient operations, reliable financial reporting, and compliance with applicable laws and regulations. Internal control standards provide a framework for identifying and addressing major performance challenges and areas at greatest risk for mismanagement. GAO, *Internal Control Standards: Internal Control Management and Evaluation Tool,* GAO-01-1008G (Washington, D.C.: August 2001).

[47] GAO, *Medicare Recovery Audit Contracting: Weaknesses Remain in Addressing Vulnerabilities to Improper Payments, Although Improvements Made to Contractor Oversight,* GAO-10-143 (Washington, D.C.: Mar. 31, 2010).

[48] GAO-10-43.

[49] HHS-OIG, *Addressing Vulnerabilities Reported by Medicare Benefit Integrity Contractors*, OEI-03-10-00500 (December 2011).

In: Fraud Detection and Deterrence ...
Editor: Anton Ferilli
ISBN: 978-1-62417-658-6

Chapter 8

STATEMENT OF DR. PETER BUDETTI, DIRECTOR, CENTER FOR PROGRAM INTEGRITY, DEPARTMENT OF HEALTH AND HUMAN SERVICES. HEARING ON "ASSESSING MEDICARE AND MEDICAID PROGRAM INTEGRITY"*

Chairman Platts, Ranking Member Towns, and Members of the Subcommittee, thank you for the invitation to discuss the Centers for Medicare & Medicaid Services' (CMS) program integrity efforts for the Medicare and Medicaid programs.

The Administration has made important strides in reducing fraud, waste and improper payments across the government. Over the last two years, CMS has implemented powerful new anti-fraud tools provided by Congress, as well as designed and implemented large-scale, innovative improvements to our Medicare and Medicaid program integrity strategy to shift beyond a "pay and chase" approach by focusing new attention on preventing fraud. Simultaneously, CMS is using the same innovative tools to further enhance our collaboration with our law enforcement partners in detecting and preventing fraud.

---

* This is an edited, reformatted and augmented version of testimony given on June 7, 2012 before the House Committee on Oversight and Government Reform, Subcommittee on Government Organization, Efficiency, and Financial Management.

Preventing and Detecting Fraud in Medicare

CMS directly administers Medicare through contracts with private companies that process claims for Medicare benefits. Every workday, Medicare pays out more than $1 billion from some 4.5 million claims, and is statutorily required to pay claims quickly, usually within 14 to 30 days. Preventing fraud in Medicare involves striking an important balance: protecting beneficiary access to necessary health care services and reducing the administrative burden on legitimate providers, while ensuring that taxpayer dollars are not lost to fraud, waste, and abuse.

CMS is using many of the new anti-fraud authorities provided in the Affordable Care Act (P.L. 111-148 and P.L. 111-152) and the Small Business Jobs Act of 2010 (P.L.111- 240) to strategically combat fraud, waste, and abuse, and is integrating additional tools into our current program integrity efforts. These new tools and authorities support our comprehensive strategy to prevent and detect fraud and abuse. These tools and authorities also require CMS to work closely with States, our law enforcement partners, the private sector, and health care providers. These efforts to date have resulted in record monetary recoveries of health care fraud and a more than 75 percent increase in defendants charged in criminal fraud cases, increasing from 797 individuals in 2008 to 1,430 last year. I am confident that the improvements we have put in place over the past two years will provide increasingly greater protections to Medicare and Medicaid for a long time to come.

The New "Twin Pillar" Strategy

Building upon our traditional program integrity efforts that focus on detecting and prosecuting fraud, CMS has implemented a twin pillar approach to fraud prevention in Medicare. The first pillar is the new Fraud Prevention System (FPS), which applies predictive analytic technology on claims prior to payment to identify aberrant and suspicious billing patterns. The second pillar is the Automated Provider Screening (APS) system, which identifies ineligible providers or suppliers prior to their enrollment or revalidation. Together these innovative new systems, the FPS and APS, are growing in their capacity to protect patients and taxpayers from those intent on defrauding our programs. These pillars represent an integrated approach to program integrity – preventing fraud before payments are made, keeping bad providers and suppliers out of Medicare in the first place, and quickly removing wrongdoers from the program once they are detected.

The First Pillar: The Fraud Prevention System

The FPS is the predictive analytic technology required under the Small Business Jobs Act. Since June 30, 2011, the FPS has been running predictive algorithms and other sophisticated analytics nationwide against all Medicare fee-for-service and durable medical equipment, prosthetics, orthotics, and supplies (DMEPOS) claims prior to payment. CMS is well ahead of the statutory implementation schedule, which called for phasing in the technology in the 10 highest fraud States in the Medicare fee-for-service program by July 1, 2011. Nationwide implementation of the technology maximizes the benefits of the FPS and permitted CMS to efficiently integrate the technology into the Medicare fee-for-service program and train our anti-fraud contractors.

CMS uses the FPS to target investigative resources to suspect claims and providers, and swiftly impose administrative action when warranted. The system generates alerts in priority order, allowing program integrity analysts to further investigate the most egregious, suspect, or aberrant activity. CMS and our program integrity contractors use the FPS to stop, prevent, and identify improper payments using a variety of administrative tools and actions, including claim denials, payment suspensions, revocation of Medicare billing privileges, and referrals to law enforcement. Under the direction of CMS' Center for Program Integrity (CPI), Zone Program Integrity Contractors (ZPICs):

- Develop investigative leads generated by the FPS and perform data analysis to identify cases of suspected fraud, waste, and abuse;
- Make recommendations to CMS for appropriate administrative actions to protect Medicare Trust Fund dollars;
- Make referrals to law enforcement for potential prosecution and provide support for ongoing investigations; and
- Identify improper payments to be recovered.

In the first ten months of implementation of the FPS, 1010 active ZPIC investigations have been supported by leads generated by the FPS. Specifically, the FPS directly resulted in 591 new investigations, while also supporting 419 pre-existing investigations. CMS is currently identifying the range of performance metrics that will fully capture the success of the FPS, and this fall, a report to Congress about the first implementation year of the FPS will describe these metrics.

Additionally, the FPS has led to 550 direct interviews with providers suspected of participating in fraudulent activity, and over 1,541 interviews with beneficiaries to confirm whether they received services for which the Medicare program had been billed. These numbers are increasing every day. The beneficiary interviews are similar to the inquiries credit card companies make to cardholders when a suspicious purchase is flagged. CMS uses the information learned from these beneficiary interviews along with historical claims data to identify the characteristics of potentially bad actors and then builds that information into the FPS's predictive algorithms and other sophisticated analytics. Additionally, CMS incorporates beneficiary complaints about potential fraudulent providers submitted via 1-800-MEDICARE directly into the FPS to further refine our analytics.

For the first time in the history of the program, CMS is using a system to apply advanced analytics against Medicare fee-for-service claims on a streaming, national basis. This has enabled CMS to identify schemes operating across Medicare Parts A and B claims and across the country. The FPS aggregates Parts A and B claims in near-real time, and this comprehensive view of claims is revolutionizing our program integrity work. For example, ZPIC investigators formerly had to check multiple systems to determine whether a beneficiary ever visited the doctor who billed Medicare for services and supplies. The FPS has consolidated the dispersed pieces of claims data – beneficiary visits with a doctor or orders for DMEPOS billed under Part B, and hospital and other provider services billed under Part A – enabling ZPICs to automatically see the full picture. Equally important, the FPS organizes the data to quickly show when two providers on opposite ends of the country are billing Medicare on behalf of the same beneficiary, rooting out potential compromised beneficiary numbers and other fraudulent activity.

The Second Pillar: Enhanced Provider Enrollment and Automated Provider Screening

The second pillar of CMS' program integrity strategy is enhanced enrollment and screening requirements for providers and suppliers seeking to enroll or revalidate their enrollment in Medicare. This innovative approach is designed to leverage the increased scrutiny applied to bad actors while simultaneously making it easier and more efficient for legitimate providers and suppliers to enroll or re-enroll in the Medicare program. CMS launched the APS technology on December 31, 2011. Medicare Administrative Contractors (MACs) and the National Supplier Clearinghouse (NSC) for DMEPOS enrollment are responsible for provider and supplier enrollment. Historically, the MACs and the NSC have processed paper applications and crosschecked information manually against various databases to verify provider and supplier enrollment requirements such as licensure status. Today, CMS is using the new APS technology to conduct routine and automated screening checks of providers and suppliers against thousands of private and public databases to more efficiently identify and remove ineligible providers and suppliers from Medicare. CMS anticipates that the new process will decrease the application processing time for providers and suppliers, while enabling CMS to continuously monitor the accuracy of its enrollment data and to assess applicants' risk to the program using standard analyses of provider and supplier data.

Provider enrollment is the gateway to the Medicare program, and CMS has made significant improvements that have begun to change the way providers and suppliers interact with CMS. The Provider Enrollment, Chain, and Ownership System (PECOS) maintains the official record of information for all providers, suppliers, and associated groups enrolled in Medicare. Provider enrollment data is used for claims payment, fraud prevention initiatives, and law enforcement activities. A key strategy for improving the process for honest providers, while clamping down on bad actors, is the creation of an all-digital process for web-based PECOS. CMS has already implemented the web-based payment of the application fee and now permits the use of electronic signatures on applications. The availability of the electronic signature option eliminates the requirement that providers and suppliers mail a paper signature at the end of the application process. As a result, CMS has seen a significant increase in the submission of web applications, especially for institutional providers, group practices, and DMEPOS suppliers.

The APS technology complements our approach to implementing the enhanced screening requirements enacted in the Affordable Care Act. This new screening strategy is tailored to both categorical and individual provider risk, rather than a one-size-fits-all approach. Categories of providers and suppliers in the "moderate" level of risk are now required to undergo an on-site visit prior to enrolling or upon revalidation of their Medicare billing privileges. This new requirement expanded on-site visits to many providers and suppliers that were previously not subject to such site visits as a requirement for enrolling in the Medicare program. In addition to announced and unannounced site visits, providers and suppliers who are designated in the "high" level of risk will be subject to fingerprint-based criminal background checks. As a result of the new Affordable Care Act screening requirements, CMS estimates that approximately 50,000 additional site visits will be conducted between March 2011 and March 2015 to ensure providers and suppliers are operational and meet certain enrollment requirements.

CMS completed the procurement of a national site visit contractor to increase efficiency and standardization of the site visits and the contractor recently started performing these site visits. The National Site Visit Contractor (NSVC) began performing site visits in late January 2012. As of April 30, 2012 the NSVC completed 6,871 site visits; of those completed, the NSVC determined 223 sites to be nonoperational; those enrollments were either denied or revoked as deemed appropriate.

CMS has embarked on an ambitious project to revalidate the enrollments of all existing 1.5 million Medicare suppliers and providers by 2015 under the new Affordable Care Act screening requirements. Since March 25, 2011, CMS enrolled or revalidated enrollment information for approximately 275,439 Medicare providers and suppliers under the enhanced screening requirements of the Affordable Care Act. These efforts will ensure that only qualified and legitimate providers and suppliers can provide health care items and services to Medicare beneficiaries.

The FPS, APS, and other enrollment enhancements promote synergy in CMS program integrity activities. For example, based on FPS leads, CMS identified specific providers and suppliers as top priorities for revalidation. As a result of screening providers and suppliers that pose an elevated risk as identified by the FPS, CMS has moved to revoke and deactivate the billing privileges and enrollment records of providers and suppliers that do not meet current Medicare enrollment requirements. The first phase of revalidation led to 13,066 deactivations of provider practice locations for non-response to the revalidation request, as of March 1, 2012. The second phase of revalidation has resulted in the deactivation of 6,278 provider enrollments records for non-response and 4,319 revocations after it was determined the providers were not properly licensed in the state in which they were enrolled, as of May 1, 2012.[1] These initiatives complement the traditional program integrity work and additional provider enrollment enhancements that CMS continues to implement.

Preventing and Detecting Fraud in Medicaid

As a State-based program, Medicaid is administered very differently than Medicare. However many of the tools CMS is applying in Medicare are being evaluated for use in Medicaid. CMS is collaborating with our State partners to ensure that those caught defrauding Medicare will not be able to defraud Medicaid, and those identified as fraudsters in one State will not be able to replicate their scams in another State's Medicaid program. Specifically, the Affordable Care Act and CMS' implementing regulations require States to terminate from Medicaid providers or suppliers who have been revoked by Medicare, or terminated for cause by another State's Medicaid program or the Children's Health Insurance Program (CHIP). Similarly, under current authority, Medicare may also revoke providers or suppliers that have been terminated by State Medicaid agencies or CHIP.

To support State efforts to share such information, CMS implemented a web-based application that allows States to share information regarding terminated providers and to view information on Medicare providers and suppliers that have had their billing privileges revoked for cause. We are confident that this interactive tool for States is the beginning of a smarter, more efficient Federal-State partnership, integrating technology solutions to routinely share relevant program information in a collaborative effort.

CMS is also actively pursuing ways to apply advanced data analytics technology, including predictive analytics, to the Medicaid program. CMS is required, under the Small Business Jobs Act of 2010, to complete an analysis of the cost-effectiveness and feasibility of expanding predictive analytics technology to Medicaid and CHIP after the third implementation year of the FPS. Based on this analysis, the law requires CMS to expand predictive analytics to Medicaid and CHIP by April 1, 2015. Although Medicaid is administered and organized in a distinctly different way than Medicare, we believe there are opportunities to transfer the knowledge and lessons learned through the FPS and APS in Medicare to States for use in Medicaid. For example, we are currently working to identify specific FPS algorithms that are relevant to Medicaid and will be performing an analysis of one State's Medicaid claims data using the identified algorithms. Once the analysis is complete, we will share the results back with the State. We anticipate the analysis being complete before the end of the year. As another example, we are partnering with the same State to screen all of the State's Medicaid providers using the APS. Once the analysis is complete, we will provide the results back to the State for their action as appropriate. The goal of this test project is to demonstrate the utility of using an automated screening application to screen Medicaid providers, and we expect results later this year. While both of the initiatives described above involve only a few States, once we test the effectiveness of these types of solutions in Medicaid, our goal is to expand these capabilities to more States. CMS is also supporting States' use of predictive analytics through technical assistance and education, including specific coursework focused on predictive analytics at the Medicaid Integrity Institute.

CMS Collaboration with States on Medicaid Program Integrity

States have primary responsibility for policing fraud, waste, and abuse in their Medicaid programs, and they have significant financial interest in doing so as they pay, on average, 43 percent of the cost of the program. However, CMS also has a significant role to play, providing technical assistance, guidance, and oversight in the State-based efforts. Section 1936 of the Social Security Act provides CMS with the authorities to fight fraud and abuse by Medicaid providers by requiring CMS to contract with private sector entities to review provider claims data, audit providers, identify overpayments, and educate providers and other individuals about payment integrity and quality of care. CMS works with partner agencies at the Federal and State levels to enhance these efforts, including preventing the enrollment of individuals and organizations that would abuse or defraud the Medicaid program and removing fraudulent or abusive providers when detected.

Because of Medicaid's structure as a Federal-State partnership, CMS has developed initiatives that are specifically designed to assist States in strengthening their own efforts to combat fraud, waste, and abuse. One of CMS' most significant achievements is the Medicaid Integrity Institute (MII), which provides for the continuing education of State program integrity employees. At the MII, CMS has a unique opportunity to offer substantive training, technical assistance, and support to States in a structured learning environment. From its inception in 2008 through May 2012, CMS has continually offered MII courses and trained more than 3,000 State employees at no cost to the States. These State employees are able to learn and share information with program integrity staff from other States on topics such as emerging trends in Medicaid Fraud, data collection, and fraud detection skills, along with other helpful topics. In 2012, CMS has already held several events at the MII and plans to host a Data Expert Symposium this summer to bring together State Medicaid data experts to exchange ideas about predictive analytics, including algorithm development and trend analysis.[2]

Just recently, CMS announced another initiative to assist States in their program integrity efforts. On May 30th, we launched the "CMS Provider Screening Innovator Challenge." This Challenge addresses our goals of improving our abilities to streamline operations, screen providers, and reduce fraud and abuse. Specifically, the Challenge is an innovation competition to develop a multi-State, multi-program provider screening software application which would be capable of risk scoring, credentialing validation, identity authentication, and sanction checks, while lowering burden on providers and reducing administrative and infrastructure expenses for States and Federal programs. Further information about the Challenge is available at www.medicaid.gov.

CMS also provides States assistance with "boots on the ground" for targeted special investigative activities. Since October 2007, CMS has participated in 12 projects in three States, with the majority occurring in Florida. CMS assisted States in the review of 654 providers, 43 home health agencies and DMEPOS suppliers, 52 group homes, and 192 assisted living facilities. During those reviews, CMS and States interviewed 1,150 beneficiaries and States took more than 540 actions against non-compliant providers (including, but not limited to fines, suspensions, licensing referrals, and State Medicaid Fraud Control Unit (MFCU) referrals). States reported these reviews have resulted in $40 million in savings through cost avoidance.

CMS Redesign of the Medicaid National Audit Program

Since the Medicaid Integrity Program is a fairly new program, we have had the opportunity to learn important lessons during the initial program years. Beginning in early 2010, CMS determined through internal analysis, environmental assessments, parallel discussions with stakeholders, and reviews of contractor performance that the initial auditing model of the Medicaid Integrity Program required fundamental changes in how it conducts its work in order to effectively support States in their efforts to combat fraud, waste, and abuse in their Medicaid programs. The 2010 Annual Report to Congress[3] on the Medicaid Integrity Program contained a section entitled "Redesign of the National Audit Program" that described how CMS was approaching improvements to Medicaid program integrity. An integral change in that redesign was the new focus on collaborative auditing projects with the

States, which moved away from traditional stand-alone Federal audits that relied on post-pay data intended largely for research purposes[4] and moved to using more timely claims data residing with each state's Medicaid Management Information System (MMIS).

As the Department of Health and Human Services' Office of Inspector General (HHS-OIG), Government Accountability Office (GAO), and our own internal assessments have identified, audits based solely on post-payment data with little input from States have had mixed results. As such, since February 2011, CMS has focused on developing collaborative audits, which allows CMS to work alongside the States in identifying areas that warrant further investigation and deserve auditing. Through this process CMS can come alongside to support a State's program integrity efforts, and in most cases, use or supplement data from a State's MMIS. The number of collaborative audits have progressively increased and since February 2011. CMS no longer assigns audits to contractors based on the results of algorithms that were developed solely using CMS Medicaid Statistical Information System (MSIS) data.

Since the earliest collaborative audits were assigned to Medicaid Integrity Contractors (MICs) in January 2010, CMS has worked with States to develop and assign 137 collaborative audits in 15 States that collectively represent approximately 53 percent of all Medicaid expenditures in FY 2011. To continue towards expanding collaborative audit projects to a broader number of States, CMS is in discussions with 15 additional States that make up approximately 26 percent of FY 2011 Medicaid expenditures. For these collaborative audits, CMS and its contractors are working with each State to develop the audit targets. In addition, the corresponding data for the collaborative audits is in many cases provided or supplemented by the States, making the data more complete and thus, increasing the accuracy of any audit findings.

CMS has continued to identify additional opportunities for program changes and improvement. CMS' redesign plan for Medicaid program integrity recognizes the significant emergence of Medicaid managed care penetration, anticipated growth in enrollment in the Medicaid program, the influence of new State Medicaid recovery audit contractors, as well as the need to eliminate certain redundant, ineffective, and inefficient practices. We are working within CMS and with our State partners to develop and test best practice approaches to managed care program integrity oversight that considers both the growth in enrollment and alternative funding arrangements.

As noted earlier, in addition to our own internal analysis, others came to many of the same conclusions for the need for changes to strengthen Medicaid program integrity. Recently, the HHS OIG,[5] the Medicaid and CHIP Payment and Access Commission (MACPAC),[6] the National Association of Medicaid Directors (NAMD),[7] and GAO[8] have identified many of these same factors and have made recommendations for changes to the Medicaid Integrity Program that parallel CMS' internal assessments and plans for restructuring the program. We appreciate the work of our partners and have taken their recommendations into consideration as we make ongoing changes to improve the program integrity efforts in our programs.

CMS is implementing the program redesign as a phased approach that involves piloting new concepts and sharing best practices with States, as well as total or supplementary use of direct State data for Medicaid Integrity Program audits. Meanwhile, CMS is working vigorously to reconfigure how to best review and audit Medicaid providers through our contractors. This reconfiguration includes expanding that review to include improving oversight of managed care entities, improving identification of audit targets like high-risk providers serving both Medicare and Medicaid beneficiaries, overhauling CMS' contractor structure, and enhancing support to States in their recovery of overpayments.

We are poised to expand the focus of our program integrity and oversight efforts. Specifically, we are expanding our program integrity efforts to address the growth of managed care in the States and the anticipated enrollment increase that will occur in 2014. In addition, as payment and service delivery reform methods are designed and implemented, we will work closely with our State partners to incorporate program integrity from the beginning. We are also working with our State partners on strategies to share information across programs and States about predicative analytics findings, terminated providers, and best practices.

Improving Data to Fight Fraud in Medicare and Medicaid

CMS has made significant improvements to our databases and analytical systems in recent years. However, we acknowledge that more can be done. CMS is committed to enhancing the quality and availability of our data to States as the agency and law enforcement continue to coordinate efforts, identify criminals, and prevent fraud on a system-wide basis. These efforts are being conducted in accordance with Affordable Care Act requirements for the centralization of certain claims data from Medicare, Medicaid, CHIP, the

Department of Veterans Affairs, the Department of Defense, the Social Security Administration, and the Indian Health Service.

CMS continues to build the Integrated Data Repository (IDR) to provide a comprehensive view of Medicare and Medicaid data including claims, beneficiary data, and drug information. The IDR provides broader and easier access to data and enhanced data integration while strengthening and supporting CMS' analytical capabilities. The IDR is currently populated with seven years of historical Medicare Parts A, B, and D paid claims, and CMS is actively working to integrate pre-payment claims data.

CMS is also working to incorporate State Medicaid data into the IDR, while also working with States to improve the quality and consistency of the MSIS data from each State. MSIS data is the primary data source for Medicaid statistical data, and is a subset of Medicaid eligibility and claims data from all 50 States and the District of Columbia. To improve the quality of the MSIS data, and Medicaid data in general, CMS established the Medicaid and CHIP Business Information Solution (MACBIS) Council. This Council provides leadership and guidance in support of efforts to create a more robust and comprehensive information management strategy for Medicaid and CHIP. The council's strategy includes:

- Promoting consistent leadership on key challenges facing State health programs;
- Improving the efficiency and effectiveness of the Federal-State partnership;
- Making data on Medicaid, CHIP, and State health programs more widely available to stakeholders; and
- Reducing duplicative efforts within CMS and minimizing the burden on States.

The Council has initiated several efforts including the Transformed MSIS (T-MSIS) pilot project in 11 States, which together represent 40 percent of the nation's Medicaid expenditures. The heart of this pilot is to create a consolidated format from a variety of State information sources to satisfy multiple Medicaid and CHIP Federal information reporting requirements. CMS will use the results and lessons learned from these 11 States as the basis for national implementation by 2014. The MACBIS projects will lead to the development and deployment of improvements in data quality and availability for Medicaid program administration, oversight, and program integrity. Improved data will allow CMS to analyze information from throughout the claims process to identify previously undetected indicators of aberrant activity. Used with the IDR, CMS' One Program Integrity (One PI) web-based portal helps CMS share data with our integrity contractors and law enforcement. The portal provides a single access point to the data within the IDR, as well as analytic tools to review the data. CMS has been working closely with our law enforcement colleagues to provide One PI training and support. Since October of 2010, CMS has trained a total of 622 program integrity contractors and CMS staff, including 82 law enforcement personnel, on the portal and tools on One PI.

CMS continues to improve access to better quality Medicaid data by exploring opportunities to collaborate with States participating in the Medicare-Medicaid Data Match Expansion Project (Medi-Medi) as well as working directly with States to obtain Medicaid data for specific collaborative projects. As these efforts mature, we expect to be able to more easily transfer the lessons learned from Medicare program integrity analytics and algorithms, including predictive analytics, to the Medicaid Integrity Program. Like in Medicare, CMS' ultimate goal is to utilize predictive modeling to enhance our analytic capabilities, as well as increase information-sharing and collaboration among State Medicaid agencies to detect and deter aberrant billing and servicing patterns at the State level and on a regional or national scale.

Looking Forward

Medicare and Medicaid fraud affect every American by draining critical resources from our health care system, and contributing to the rising cost of health care for all. The Administration has made a firm commitment to rein in fraud, waste and improper payments. Today, we have more tools than ever before to move beyond "pay and chase" and implement strategic changes in pursuing and detecting fraud, waste, and abuse. I look forward to continuing to work with you as we make improvements in protecting the integrity of Federal health care programs and safeguarding taxpayer resources.

End Notes

[1] We note that the first and second phase revalidation results are preliminary results as deactivated providers could reactivate over time with updated practice information or after showing evidence of proper licensing.

[2] Medicaid Integrity Institute FY-12Training Calendar: http://www.justice.gov/usao/eousa/ole/mii/mii.courses.12.pdf

[3] http://www.cms.gov/Regulations-and-Guidance/Legislation/DeficitReductionAct/Downloads/fy10rtc.pdf; page 24.

[4] MSIS data is the primary data source for Medicaid statistical data, and is a subset of Medicaid eligibility and claims data from all 50 States and the District of Columbia.

[5] HHS OIG, "Early Assessment of Audit Medicaid Integrity Contractors." March 2012. http://oig.hhs.gov/oei/reports/oei-05-10-00210.pdf

[6] MACPAC, "Report to the Congress on Medicaid and CHIP." March 2012. http://www.macpac.gov/reports/2012-03-15_MACPAC_Report.pdf?attredirects=0&d=1

[7] NAMD, "Rethinking Medicaid Program Integrity: Eliminating Duplication and Investing in Effective, High-Value Tools." March 2012. http://medicaiddirectors.org/sites/medicaiddirectors.org/files/public/namd_medicaid_pi_position_paper_final_12031 9.pdf

[8] GAO. "Medicare and Medicaid Fraud, Waste, and Abuse: Effective Implementation of Recent Laws and Agency Actions Could Health Reduce Improper Payments." March 2011. http://www.gao.gov/assets/130/125646.pdf

INDEX

E

F

G

H

I

S

T